Moses, Jesus, and the Trickster
in the Evangelical South

Moses, Jesus, and the Trickster
in the Evangelical South

PAUL HARVEY

Mercer University Lamar Memorial Lectures No. 52

THE UNIVERSITY OF GEORGIA PRESS   Athens and London

Paperback edition, 2013
© 2012 by the University of Georgia Press
Athens, Georgia 30602
www.ugapress.org
All rights reserved
Set in Sabon and Filosofia by Graphic Composition, Inc.

Printed digitally in the United States of America

The Library of Congress has cataloged the
hardcover edition of this book as follows:
Harvey, Paul, 1961–
Moses, Jesus, and the trickster in the evangelical South / Paul Harvey.
xi, 182 p. : ill. ; 23 cm. —
(Mercer University Lamar memorial lectures ; no. 52)
Includes bibliographical references (p. 159–172) and index.
ISBN-13: 978-0-8203-3411-0 (cloth : alk. paper)
ISBN-10: 0-8203-3411-1 (cloth : alk. paper)
1. Southern States—Church history. 2. Evangelicalism—
Southern States—History. 3. Christianity and culture—
Southern States—History. 4. Race relations—
Religious aspects—Protestant churches—History.
5. Southern States—Race relations—History.
6. Tricksters—Southern States. I. Title.
BR535.H385 2011
280'.40975—dc23
2011030208

Paperback ISBN-13: 978-0-8203-4592-5
ISBN-10: 0-8203-4592-X

British Library Cataloging-in-Publication Data available

For my teachers at Oklahoma Baptist University
and the University of California at Berkeley.

And

for friends and colleagues in the
Lilly Fellows Program,
Valparaiso University.

Contents

Acknowledgments ix
A Note on Illustrations and Endnotes xi

INTRODUCTION.
What Is the Soul of Man?
1

CHAPTER ONE.
Moses, Jesus, Absalom, and the Trickster:
Narratives of the Evangelical South
6

CHAPTER TWO.
"'Because I Was a Master'":
Religion, Race, and Southern Ideas of Freedom
54

CHAPTER THREE.
Suffering Saint: Jesus in the South
96

Notes 159
Index 173

Acknowledgments

This book derives from three lectures originally delivered as the Lamar Lectures in Southern History at Mercer University in early November 2008, just as a historical presidential election was taking place. For their warm cordiality and support, I want to thank Sarah Gardner, Douglas Thompson, and the others on the Lamar Lecture Committee who arranged for this series of exploratory talks. Thanks also to Bill Underwood, president of Mercer University, who arranged a postlecture election-watching party at his presidential house at Mercer.

For their ongoing collegiality, advice, and research tips, I owe much to Edward J. Blum, Randall Stephens, Matt Sutton, Kathryn Lofton, Rebecca Goetz, Kelly J. Baker, Philip Goff, Kevin Schultz, Mike Pasquier, Lin Fisher, and David Sehat.

I have dedicated this book to my undergraduate and graduate teachers. As a product of a denominational liberal arts college and a major public university, benefiting since from postdoctoral work at a midsized church-related university and currently blessed with generous and supportive colleagues at a smaller state university campus, I've been fortunate enough to experience many sides of the American higher education system. I especially want to thank my college teachers Dale Soden, the late Laura Crouch, the late Gerry Gunnin, James Farthing, and John Mayer; my graduate school teachers Leon Litwack, James Gregory, the late Reginald Zelnick, and the late William Shack; my Lilly Fellow colleagues John Fea, Joe Creech, Mark Schwehn, Arlin Meyer, "Buzz" Berg, Jon Pahl, Darren Dochuk, Stephanie Paulsell, and Pamela Parker; and my colleagues in the History Department at the University of Colorado at Colorado Springs, especially Rob Sackett, Christina Jiménez, and Christopher Hill.

A Note on Illustrations and Endnotes

This book includes references to maps (in chapter 1) and to paintings and other illustrations (in chapter 3) that are best viewed in color. Because illustrations included in this book had to be reproduced in black and white, I have created an accompanying website at http://paulharvey.org/moses; it includes a full list of web addresses where readers may view the illustrations in color. I encourage readers to use the link especially when reading about the illustrations discussed in chapter 3, as color is central to understanding these paintings, photographs, and drawings.

Throughout the book I will include references to URLs for the maps and paintings. Because web addresses can be transitory, a full updated list of these URLs will be kept at the accompanying website, and when permissions can be obtained, the illustrations also will be available on the website.

Because this book constitutes the published form of a series of lectures meant to be suggestive and informal more than scholarly and definitive, many arguments and assertions that normally would be accompanied by copious endnotes listing relevant sources in the primary and secondary literature are not present. I have chosen instead to supply references mostly when I use direct quotations, and I ask readers to assume that the arguments made in the book come from years of reading and thinking about the subject.

Moses, Jesus, and the Trickster in the Evangelical South

INTRODUCTION

What Is the Soul of Man?

Won't somebody tell me, answer if you can!
Want somebody tell me, what is the soul of a man
I'm going to ask the question, answer if you can
If anybody here can tell me, what is the soul of a man?
I've traveled in different countries, I've traveled foreign lands
I've found nobody to tell me, what is the soul of a man

When the pioneering gospel blues slide guitarist Blind Willie Johnson recorded "What Is the Soul of Man?" for Columbia records in the late 1920s, he challenged listeners to ponder a question central to the religious experience. The Texan used his growling voice to pose religious queries and challenges, as in "John the Revelator":

> Who's that writing? John the Revelator.
> Who's that writing? John the Revelator.
> Who's that writing? John the Revelator.
> Hey! Book of the Seventh Seal.

Johnson's evangelical self-examination, "Nobody's Fault but Mine," has been covered numerous times since.

The gospel blues originating in the interwar years typically expressed optimistic verities about a Jesus who was real. Johnson's grittier, sometimes apocalyptic songs rarely provide such assurance. "What Is the Soul of Man?" challenges the idea that man is only the physical material of the brain, for the resurrection of Jesus proves that "man is more than his mind." Beyond that, the soul of man remains a mystery.

This book tours some of the answers Protestants in the American South historically have given to the philosophical quandary posed by Blind Willie Johnson. How did southern Protestants, black and white, from the eighteenth century to the civil rights era, grapple with the intractable religious and philosophical questions through religious expression and belief? How did they come to terms with questions about the soul of man? Most particularly, how did they do so through religious institutions, thought, and culture? How did they do so through theology, folklore, music, art, drama, and film? And why did their cultural expressions of religious faith characteristically take on an intensity and vivacity that continues to attract our attention today, giving the South its Bible Belt image?

Based on three public lectures given at Mercer University in the fall of 2008, this short book examines Bible stories as they were transmitted in the South alongside historical understandings from Wilbur J. Cash forward, literary evocations of religion in the region (focusing especially on William Faulkner, Toni Morrison, and Edward P. Jones), musical expressions, film, and art. The aim is for a brief, evocative exploration of key expressions of religious culture in the South, one that engages both historical narrative and literary/artistic/sonic expression.

Ultimately, *Moses, Jesus, and the Trickster* explores further whether "southern evangelicalism" is capacious enough to capture the complex religious life of Christians in the region. When southerners have examined the soul of man, they have come up with a variety of answers belying the simple reliance on evangelical archetypes. In other words, when we move beyond formal theological statements, electoral maps, and data collection, we find a capacious religious experience belying simple stereotypes about southern religion. Answers to Blind Willie Johnson's question may be gleaned by focusing on some of the central symbolic figures of southern religious history.

To understand fully how southern believers have defined the soul of man, we must broaden our field of vision beyond the usual suspects in the study of southern religion. Here we will do so through an examination of four historical literary archetypes: Moses, Jesus, the Trickster, and Absalom. Moses and Jesus are familiar, Absalom and the Trickster less so, yet they too have been formative to creating the southern sacred. Southerners' answers to questions about the soul of man suggest the power of evangelical Protestantism in southern history, as well as the ways in which that power consistently has been challenged and questioned. Skeptics have nibbled around the edges of the evangelical culture that came to cultural dominance after the Civil War. Literary figures, cultural archetypes, and musical explorations have added layers of cultural complexity to what otherwise might be seen as a solid South of evangelicalism.

The first chapter surveys the major biblical, literary, and folkloric characters of Moses, Jesus, Absalom, and the Trickster as they have come down through the history of southern religious culture. If Moses and Jesus represent the conscious engagement of theological ideas in the South, Absalom and the Trickster speak to more subterranean elements. If Moses and Jesus are moral paragons, Absalom and the Trickster are necessary morally gray figures. Southerners required such a complex cast of characters to grapple with a social world riven with intractable conflicts.

The second chapter analyzes the social history of religious ideas of freedom in the South from the eighteenth century to the Civil War. In his recent profound work *The Myth of American Religious Freedom*, historian David Sehat has uncovered the ways Americans of all political persuasions have misunderstood or misused the history of the First Amendment and the concept of separation of church and state. He identifies a "moral establishment" that survived the wall of separation between church and state, one that was as coercive as the legal establishment it followed. Nowhere was this more true than in the South, where a moral establishment grew up alongside the institution of slavery and, indeed, provided key justifications for human bondage. With such a history, religious ideas of freedom came to have a social, not just a legal, meaning. Exploring their evolution requires understanding the social history of how they came to be developed precisely by those who were denied freedom.

The final chapter focuses more specifically on Jesus. The black birth of Jesus, the white rebirth, and the twentieth-century struggles over the imagery of Jesus suggest how and why Christ came to be especially associated with the South. This chapter continues also the story of the evolution of religious ideas of freedom through the twentieth century into the civil rights era, completing the narrative begun in chapter two. The figure of Jesus became central to those ideas of freedom.

As a preface and apologia, an explanation of what is not here. Perhaps most importantly, there is comparatively little about the Catholic South and, therefore, not as much about Louisiana and New Orleans as one might wish. This book makes no pretense of covering the religion of Native peoples. Further, it deals only tangentially with the recent diversification of religion in the South, including the migration of Latinos and Asians to a region historically dominated by people of English/Scots Irish origin and people of African descent. This runs counter to much contemporary scholarship in American religious history. Recent work in this field has pushed toward understanding pluralism, to "decentering the narrative," to incorporating the stories and religious traditions of those historically ignored in the dominant consensus historiography, and to examining alternative religious traditions. Historians have urged an understanding of early southern religious history that does not assume evangelicalism would emerge triumphant and that places Catholicism front and center as an actor in southern religious history. Thus, the chapters that follow swim against a strong (and necessary and cleansing) tidal wave in American religious history. They are a throwback to an earlier kind of religious history that centered Protestantism and marginalized other traditions. There are obvious costs in doing this; but there are also distortions to the historical record in pretending that southern religious history was characterized by a heritage of diverse, plural, coequal religious traditions. That is just not the case. Some people had more power than others—a lot more.

In *Freedom's Coming: Religious Cultures and the Shaping of the South from the Civil War through the Civil Rights Era*, I traced the mutual influence of racism, racial interchange, and interracialism in southern religious history. Here, I want to expand further on points raised there and see what themes drawn from outside the evangelical orbit per se—namely, the figures of the Trickster and the conflicted story of Absalom—bring to the study of southern religion. We can go further. If Jesus has been a pure figure in white southern theology, he could become a trickster of the trinity in black thought and lore. If Moses has represented deliverance, then Absalom has shown how the Egyptians and the Israelites in fact were entangled in one narrative. Absalom suggests that the southern drive for purity and the obsession with miscegenation covered over the fact that no people were more impure. The design of the masters of southern history—for racial and religious purity, and for a definition of freedom that depended on order, obedience, and hierarchy—was a hoax. Throughout southern history, the soul of man has burst those bonds and produced a rich cultural history in song, sermon, art, tale, dance, and literature.

CHAPTER ONE

Moses, Jesus, Absalom, and the Trickster

Narratives of the Evangelical South

When, how, and why did the South become the Bible Belt? And why are the states considered the Bible Belt also so closely associated with high rates of violence, incarceration, divorce, alcoholism, obesity, and infant mortality? Grappling with these two questions together illuminates some basic paradoxes of southern history and something about the soul of man as well. Most especially, these questions compel us to confront the rise of evangelicalism as a dominant social force in the region simultaneous with persistent poverty and violence. Juxtaposing rates of religiosity and measurements of social ills helps frame an understanding of the religious archetypes explored through this book. They take in the precarious balance of piety and inhumanity, of Jesus and gin, and of evangelicalism and evil.

Consider first a comparison of electoral maps from 1800 and 2000. Two hundred years ago, New England was the Bible Belt, and a solid bloc of support for John Adams in the 1800 election (view the electoral map linked at this book's website, or at http://www.270towin.com/, and select the election of 1800 in the dropdown box). The South was something else. It was nothing like a Bible Belt, not with its candidate, Thomas Jefferson, being accused of religious heterodoxy and atheism. He was not an atheist, but he was no orthodox Christian either, given his scornful dismissal of the supernatural happenings of the Bible.

A dramatic contrast to the 1800 electoral map may be found in a breakdown of the concentration of Baptist churches by American counties as of 2000 based on data from the American Religious Identification Survey (ARIS) (Figure 1; this map, and others derived from the same data that also show dramatic regional variations in American patterns of religious expression and denominational concentrations, may better be viewed in color at http://www.valpo.edu/geomet/pics/geo200/religion/church_bodies.gif, and are also linked at this book's website: http://paulharvey.org/moses).

To the question, is the South still a Bible Belt, the map's obvious answer would be yes. According to the ARIS data for 2001, the South at that time had the highest percentage of churchgoers who affiliated themselves with Baptist (23.5 percent), Presbyterian (3 percent), and black Protestant (14 percent, well over half of whom are Baptists) churches. The Evangelical Belt as defined here has been, in very many counties, effectively a Baptist Belt as well; compare the presence of Baptists in the region in these data from 2001 to the 5.7 percent of New Englanders who are Baptists and the national low of 3.8 percent in the Coastal Northwest. The 2001 data also highlighted the South as counting the highest regional percentage of white non-Hispanic Methodists (6.9 percent), together with a relatively high percentage of white non-Hispanic Pentecostal/Charismatic adherents (3 percent). Moreover, in the ARIS data, the South counted the lowest numbers of respondents who answered "no religion" when asked generally about their religious beliefs and affiliations (10 percent), and nearly the lowest count for white Catholics (9.7 percent). It is little wonder that the volume of the Religion by Region series devoted to the Deep South states is titled *Religion and Public Life in the South: In the Evangelical Mode*.[1]

State-level data are equally informative. According to the North American Religion Atlas (compiled in 2000), evangelical Protestant members as a percentage of the total population by 2000 peaked in Alabama (32 percent, the highest in the region) and Mississippi (31 percent), followed closely by Tennessee (29.4 percent) and Kentucky (26.7 percent). Mainline Protestant members—a category that would include the substantial membership of United

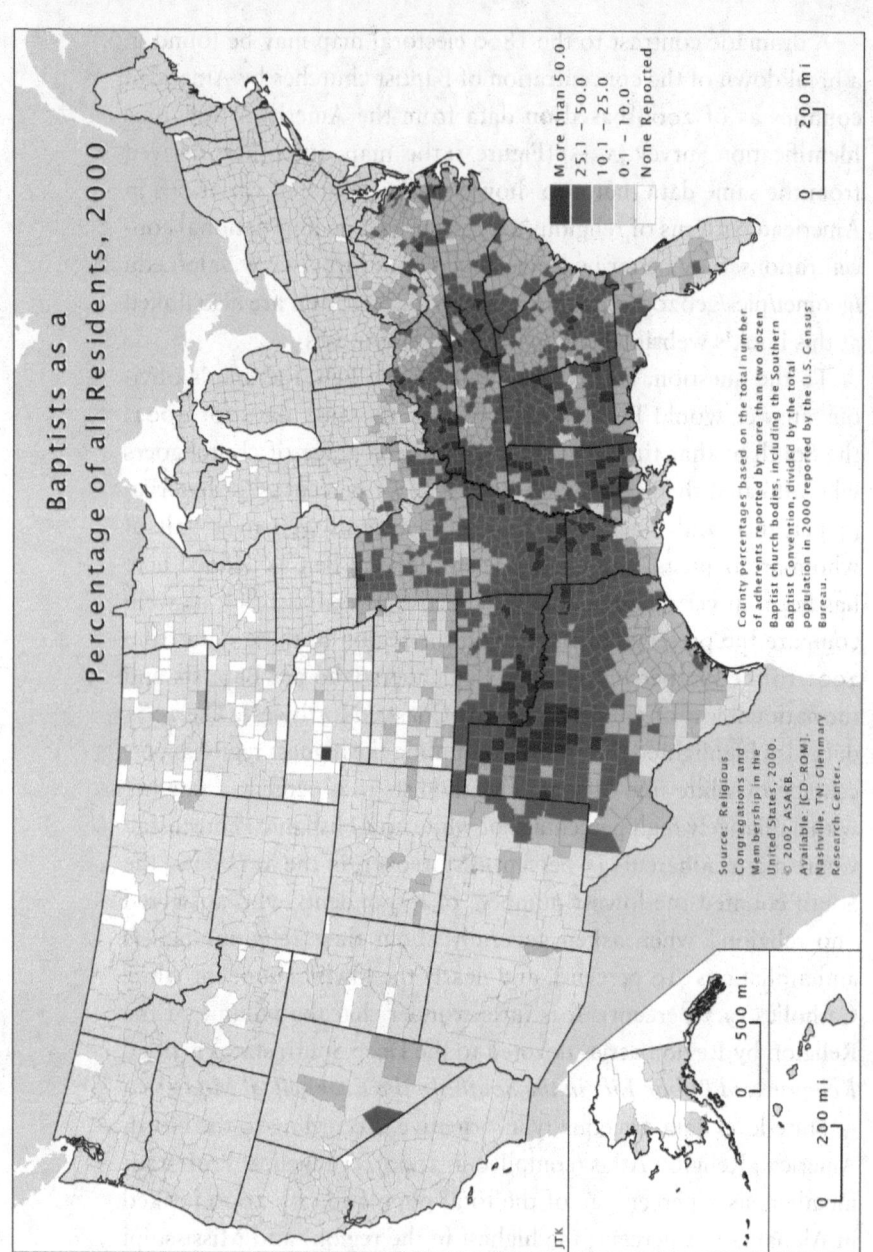

Digital map showing Baptists as percentage of residents by county, 2000.

Methodists, for example—count another 7 percent of the population of Alabama, with comparable numbers in other southern states. Of the total southern population, 19 percent were counted as Baptist adherents and 12.4 percent as historically African American Protestant. These figures compare to national counts in 2000 of Baptist members as 6.6 percent of the population, or 8.5 percent if measured in terms of adherents, and 7.4 percent of those in the historically African American Protestant category.

This is not to suggest that evangelical Protestantism has uniformly dominated the region. On the contrary, evangelical Protestant adherents as a percentage of population have been concentrated heavily in particular regions and counties, especially in a broad swath that cuts directly through the historic cotton country and some upcountry regions of the Old South. The term "Evangelical Belt" is apt, for Evangelical Protestant dominance measured by county historically has looked very much like a belt when mapped by county (albeit with a considerable belly overhang in regions of the Upper South).

A contrast of two states in the region illustrates this point clearly. In Mississippi, according to North American Religion Atlas data for 2000, Baptist adherents (excluding historically African American Protestants) included 34 percent of the total population, and historically African American Protestant adherents accounted for another 29 percent. Just over 16 percent of Mississippians were "unaffiliated" or "uncounted." Jews existed in too small a number to form even a 1 percent slice on the pie chart. Some counties of Mississippi actually had 0 percent reporting "unaffiliated" or "uncounted." In Amite County, Mississippi, for example, 44 percent of state residents counted themselves as Baptist and 42 percent as adherents to historically black churches. With Methodists at 5 percent and Mormons racking up a surprisingly high 4 percent of the county's population, Amite County in 2000 stood as one of the most religious counties in the entire United States. Virtually every individual surveyed was affiliated with or tied to some religious tradition.[2]

In Virginia, by distinct contrast, almost half the population went into the unaffiliated or uncounted category—a larger percentage than the country as a whole. Baptist adherents, excluding historically African American churches, counted for 12 percent of the state, a figure approximating the national average (in contrast to much of the rest of the South). The religiosity of Amite County, Mississippi, stood off against the relative religious indifference evidenced in Albermarle County, Virginia. The county that includes Charlottesville and the University of Virginia as its centerpiece ranked unusually high, by either regional or national standards, in the category of "unaffiliated or uncounted," almost 64 percent of its population. On the whole, Albermarle County looked more like the Pacific Northwest or other regions of relatively high levels of indifference than it looked like most southern counties.

Regional religious traditions appear even more significantly in data compiled in the 1990s by John Green of the University of Akron. In Green's survey, the South in that decade had the highest percentages of those who self-identified as "evangelical" or "historically black Protestant" (41 percent and 16 percent respectively), alongside the lowest percentages of Catholic adherents (12 percent) and of those claiming to be non-Christian or secular (12 percent). On the abortion issue, the Evangelical Belt remained solidly pro-life, by a margin of 67 percent pro-life to 33 percent pro-choice. The South as a whole led the poll in the number of people holding a "high view" of the Bible (that is, those who endorsed some variant of the statement that the Bible is the inspired Word of God). In this survey, 68 percent of southerners professed belief in the inspired Bible. All religious groups in the South—evangelical, mainline, black, Catholic, "other Christian," Jewish, and (most interestingly of all) those self-identified as "secular"—were more likely (usually considerably so) to claim a "high view" of Biblical authority. Eighty-five percent of southern evangelicals claimed a high view, as did 62 percent of mainline Protestants and 30 percent of secularists. The South, then, stood as the most solidly evangelical region of the country, and the South's evangelicals the most conservative in their voting patterns, views of biblical authority, and attitudes toward significant social issues.

One more piece of evidence confirms this conclusion: a very recent Gallup Poll survey asking "Is religion an important part of your everyday life?" Southern states comprised ten of the top eleven in the percentage of people who answered "yes":

Is Religion an Important Part of Your Daily Life

State	Percent Yes
Mississippi	85
Alabama	82
South Carolina	80
Tennessee	79
Louisiana	78
Arkansas	78
Georgia	76
North Carolina	76
Oklahoma	75
Kentucky	74
Texas	74

Thus, the history of the South from about the mid-eighteenth century to the present suggests a massive social move from (relative) indifference to piety and from enlightened rational religion to evangelical enthusiasm. Surely this is one of the most significant regional transformations in American history. An entire generation of scholarship on southern religion, epitomized most recently by Christine Heyrman's *Southern Cross: The Origins of the Bible Belt*, has examined the rise of evangelicalism as a dominant force in southern religious life. It was far from inevitable but the product of a very particular set of historical forces. These included the efforts of plain-folk Baptist, Methodist, and Presbyterian exhorters, the expansion of slavery into the newly opening Cotton Belt, the enthusiastic adoption and adaptation of Christianity by enslaved people, and the sacralization of the region through the experience of the Civil War and the postwar Lost Cause.[3]

But evangelicalism is not the only distinctive mark of the region. A second set of maps and indices suggests the converse. The region is also the gun, violence, imprisonment, illiteracy, obesity, diabetes, and early mortality belt. On nearly every negative social index, southern states rank disproportionately high and generally dominate the top ten. Southern states comprise eight of the top ten worst states in the country for murders per capita. For gun violence, southern states make up 15 of the top 24 states in gross homicide rates. For infant mortality rates, the worst twelve states are in the South. Mississippi, Louisiana, Kentucky, Oklahoma, West Virginia, and Tennessee lead the nation in obesity, with rates ranging from 30 to 35 percent. Not surprisingly, statistics for heart disease and diabetes show similar trends by state. Educational levels in the South continue to lag behind the rest of the nation, as shown in a state-by-state survey of prose literacy skills.[4]

There are exceptions. Las Vegas single-handedly lifts Nevada to its high per capita divorce rate, while some of the poorest counties in America are in South Dakota, home to the Pine Ridge Reservation. Nonetheless, on nearly every measurement, from poor health to interpersonal violence to low educational achievements, southern states fill the hall of shame. For a region that disproportionately counts "values voters" who stress the importance of "social" and "moral" issues in swaying them at the ballot box, southern states are singularly underachieving in terms of family stability, educational achievement, and personal and social health. The political rhetoric of moral values seems to crest in direct proportion to the prevalence of social ills. Thus, the least evangelical states nationally have the highest marriage and lowest divorce rates, and vice versa.

Some of these indices of social ills (especially rates of gun violence and incarceration) describe a national problem. Nonetheless, rates of religiosity and negative social indicators considered together clearly provide a social basis for the dualities that pervade southern cultural expression. Characters from Faulkner's novels, Son House's blues, and Johnny Cash's country have emerged from a southern reality of a bifurcated soul. The paradoxes and tensions between evangelicalism and evil, piety and irony, and salvation and sin are deeply rooted in American culture, but they always appear in relief through southern history.

This is why Blind Willie Johnson's question about the soul of man took on a special import in a region where that soul was so deeply and manifestly torn. Southerners historically have been forced to confront questions of poverty, interpersonal violence, social regression, and defeat, as C. Vann Woodward famously explored in *The Irony of Southern History*. Because of that, southerners have produced cultural works that plumb the depths of the human soul, and they have sketched some of our most basic understandings both of religious characters and of those who exist in the netherworld, just outside the boundaries of how Americans conventionally have defined religion. These figures, too, inhabit the sacred landscape, for they have arisen from southerners' grappling with Blind Willie Johnson's question. Moses, Jesus, Absalom, and the Trickster all play a role in answering questions about the soul of man. The remainder of this chapter tours a few of the ways southern Protestants have employed these four archetypes. Chapter 3 of this book focuses at more length specifically on the figure of Jesus, taking the material in this chapter forward through the twentieth century and into the civil rights era.

Moses, Absalom, Jesus, and the Trickster in the Slave South

Two characters from the Bible are central to the ways southerners have told about their religious experiences: Moses and Jesus. To them must be added the Trickster. In using that term, I refer to figures from the African American and European American imaginary who established a subterranean unsettling presence in southern lore, as well as to men and women who personified tricksters in their self-created artistic personae. Finally, some of the deepest and most conflicted parts of southern history may be understood through the story of Absalom, David's rebellious son killed in battle against his father. Here, we will introduce the figures of Moses, Jesus, and the Trickster as defining themes in the history of southern religion. We will also meet Absalom, taken both from the Bible; from William Faulkner's greatest novel, *Absalom, Absalom!*; and from Faulkner's black literary descendants. These four archetypes, read in the evangelical medium that pervaded the South from the late eighteenth century forward, helped southerners narrate for themselves answers to the question, what is the soul of man?

The figure of Moses suggests the ways whites saw themselves as a chosen people in suffering and war and how Africans and African Americans reworked the stories of the Bible to their own purposes. Jesus as a central religious figure rose with the spread of the evangelical South in the nineteenth century. The ghostly presence of the Trickster, hovering at the edges of the southern sacred world, directs our attention to the European American and African American popular beliefs that existed alongside Christianity, sometimes in tension and sometimes in complement. The story of David and his son Absalom narrates the biological and metaphorical relationships of whites and blacks. If Moses and Jesus were about purity and triumph, Absalom and the Trickster suggested counternarratives of impurity and ambiguity. If Moses and Jesus were about exodus and salvation, Absalom and the Trickster signified amorality, tragedy, and evil.

Moses, Jesus, Absalom, and the Trickster thus take us symbolically through the history of southern evangelical thought, practice, and expression. They also set in relief the juxtapositions traced above of piety and evil, of valor and violence, and of the sacred and southern social ills.

Moses and Jesus are the most familiar characters from the biblical stories. Both have deeply inhabited southern religious expression, appearing constantly in sermons, folklore, musical lyrics, and literary forms. Yet Moses and Jesus as archetypes are necessary but not sufficient to encompass southern religious culture. A broader cast is needed to understand southern conceptions of impurity, ambiguity, darkness, evil, and death. Further, the figure of Absalom suggests the depth of rage, violence, and guilt in southern life. Thus, Moses, Jesus, Absalom, and the Trickster considered together bring to life the range and complexity of southern conceptions of the sacred.

Even more than most places, the South stands as a land of paradox and contradiction. How else, for example, can one grasp the coexistence of barbaric rituals such as lynching and the efflorescence of literature as represented most notably by William Faulkner? How else can we explain that racial violence seemed especially vicious in counties dominated by evangelical piety? How else can we plumb a southern identity defined for so many by whiteness—by that "single resolve indomitably maintained," according to early twentieth-century historian Ulrich B. Phillips, that the South had been and would remain a "white man's country"—together with Wilbur J. Cash's observation that "Negro entered into white man as surely as white man entered into Negro—subtly influencing every gesture, every word, every emotion and idea, every attitude"? How else to match up the brilliance of southern arts both high and low with the despair of contemporaries who, like Wilbur J. Cash, characterized the "mind of the South" precisely as having no mind but rather a "savage ideal."[5]

Part of that contradiction involves the image of the South as "God-haunted," as Jesus-possessed, and at the same time as a region of slavery and apartheid. Biblical stories mixed with cultural fables and musical/artistic explorations have given southerners narratives by which to grapple with piety, salvation, evil, and mystery. These have ranged from the deeply liberatory saga of Moses to the suffering and the ultimate triumph represented in the life of Jesus, to the mysteriously hovering Trickster, to the Oedipal (and, in the South, racial) family theme told in variations of the Absalom story. Black southerners, for example, asked "what is the soul of man?" in a region where whites debated whether people of African descent possessed souls. Whites and blacks alike cast their historical experiences of wandering through deserts and searching for promised lands as replaying the story of Moses and the Israelites, and they did much the same when they sang about, depicted in painting, and retold in story and film the sufferings of Jesus.

Both black and white southerners also faced quandaries for which evangelical stories of Moses and Jesus could provide no fully satisfying narratives. In looking for answers to questions about the soul of man, they deployed a diverse array of cultural tricksters—conjure men, witches, drifters, gamblers, devils, and imagined demons, from slave conversion narratives focusing on the soul's "little me" to Johnny Cash's songs about the "beast in me." Finally, southern literary figures have played on variations of the Absalom story. They have explored Oedipal and racial rage at the mixed-up families that slavery, segregation, and miscegenation produced. If Moses and Jesus followed an arc toward justice, Absalom and the Trickster opened up narratives to grapple with mystery, impurity, hybridity, and tragedy.

Moses, Moses, Don't Get Lost

The Moses saga is a deeply rooted part of the national narrative. Moses and the Promised Land have empowered political rhetoric from John Winthrop to Thomas Jefferson, Abraham Lincoln, Ronald Reagan, and beyond. The Moses of southern religious history represents a regional variation of the national faith in America as a chosen land and Americans as a chosen people.

Stories about and analogies to Moses (and Jesus) abound in the two main examples to be explored here: slave spirituals and white southern Civil War sermons. In their own ways, both ritual incantations freely mixed stories of Moses and Jesus. Both invoked the biblical narrative of being the chosen people and wandering through a wilderness of tribulation; both spoke of finding the promised land and being with God, if only in an eschatological sense. Both, as well, freely employed Jesus to invoke blessings on the people and often portrayed Jesus as a Moses-like leader. The universality and adaptability of the biblical imagery suggests once again how common stories and myths deeply divided two people.

The common perception of southern religion ties black southerners, especially slaves, to Old Testament stories focusing on bondage and deliverance and likewise associates white southerners with a Jesus of triumph and redemption and evangelical culture. This is not wrong, but it is too simple. The powerful narratives of the Bible cut many ways. Southern evangelical believers developed a strangely conflicted relationship with Moses and this most fundamental biblical story. Who, really, were the Israelites? Who was God testing so that He could bring them to greater things in the future?

Nearly everyone now associates slave religious expression with Old Testament images of Moses leading his children to the Promised Land, of Daniel in the lion's den, of the "great vengeance and furious anger" of Ezekiel (later immortalized by Samuel Jackson's redemptive figure in *Pulp Fiction*). The slave spirituals, the martyred figures of African American religious history, and the songs of gospel choirs—these are the images and sounds that spring to mind.

Moses and the story of Exodus as a prototype of the slave experience dominate the literature of antebellum black religion. Slave spirituals sang of how "When Moses smote the water / The children all passed over / And turned back Pharaoh's army, hallelu!" Revenge for Pharaoh's deeds came in the next verse: "When Pharaoh crossed the water / The waters came together / And drowned ole Pharaoh's army, hallelu!" Slaves sang "I want to go to Canaan" and "O, remember let me go to Canaan / To meet 'em at de comin' day." They sought to be with Moses and Jesus, often conceived as two parts of the same narrative: "I wants to go where Moses trod / O de dying Lamb! / For Moses gone to de promised land / O de dying Lamb!" Brother Moses promised to be there while they drank "from streams dat never run dry."[6] As a northern army chaplain said of slaves in 1865, "Moses is their ideal of all that is high, and noble, and perfect, in man," with Christ seen "not so much in the light of a *spiritual* Deliverer, as that of a second Moses." Slave songs and lore often merged Moses and Jesus. As one verse went, "Gwine to write to Massa Jesus / To send some Valiant soldier / To turn back Pharaoh's army, Hallelu!"[7]

Black slaves easily identified with the children of Israel in bondage in Egypt. The end of the Civil War seemed to exemplify the very Exodus story of which they had sung. God had answered prayers for deliverance in sending real-life versions of Moses and Jesus. Jubilant slaves gathered around Sherman's army, one observer noted, and "to them, it was like the bondsmen going out of Egypt." With the coming of freedom and the day of jubilee, hymns of thanksgiving poured forth from churches: "Jehovah has triumphed, his people are free." An ex-slave remembered that "God planned dem slave prayers to free us like he did de Israelites, and he did." Another said, "the children of Israel was in bondage one time, and God sent Moses to 'liver them. Well, I s'pose that God sent Abe Lincoln to 'liver us."[8] Black ministers continued to preach that faith after the war, reminding congregants that "there must be no looking back to Egypt. Israel passed forty years in the wilderness, because of their unbelief. What if we cannot see right off the green fields of Canaan, Moses could not. He could not even see how to cross the Red Sea."[9]

Yet something is forgotten in this well-known account. White southerners defined themselves using the same biblical persona and the same Old Testament imagery. They did so despite their seemingly more natural resemblance to the slaveholders than to the enslaved in this story.

How did Moses become a part of the white southern mythos? Simply put, Moses and the children in bondage (and sometimes Job, the emblem of suffering) bolstered white southerners' self-understanding as a people oppressed, hemmed in on all sides, politically outnumbered, ideologically challenged and harassed, and forced to confront the prospect of dishonor. White southerners took a national story of Moses and gave it a southern twist. The Civil War, for many southern ministers, became the southern equivalent to wandering in the wilderness. Under this analogy, Moses would lead the people through their time of suffering and toward a promised land of independence and self-determination. This imagery filled sermons during the Civil War and Reconstruction, when white southerners thought they understood what it was like to be in bondage to an oppressive power.

Southern white antebellum theologians, for example, constantly referred to the Old Testament to justify slavery, putting themselves in the place of the Israelites attempting to follow God's law. The Israelites had been servants to Egyptians, but then God sent Moses to bring them out of Egypt. And through Moses, one white southern minister explained, "God gave them laws by which they were to be governed." No law coming from them could be considered wrong, for "Nothing which God ordained can be a crime." This principle included those laws from Leviticus that distinguished between bond servants and hired servants and those that advised purchasing slaves from "the heathen that are round about you" and from the children of strangers. These could be taken as bondsmen forever. As a result, even when Israelites had no slaves or use for them, God nonetheless "provided laws for bringing in, buying, inheriting and governing, slaves, in the land unto which they were to be brought at the end of forty years. He made laws recognizing the right of property, in man and in his descendants, forever—the right to trade in that property, and the right to punish the slave, with no limitation, except that if the slave should die under his master's hand, the master should be punished." Abuse of slaves was criminal, but the slave-master relation in and of itself was "good and moral." Southern thinkers pressed home the points that the Israelites did hold slaves, not just servants, and that they were governed according to Mosaic law. Thus, slavery was "positively instituted by god Himself," said one divine, to which another added, "That which is once right in the eyes of God is always right."[10] The fact that the New Testament never condemns slavery but only urges obedience from slaves further lent credence to this view, at least in the eyes of these antebellum southern theologians. The Bible, and history, were both on their side, they believed, while the tides of western civilization demolished traditional religious and political orders and threatened anarchy everywhere. Ironically, of course, in the act of secession these southern slaveholders set in motion the greatest social revolution in American history—emancipation, and the incorporation of African Americans into the body politic.[11]

The Civil War confirmed the Moses story as well, for years of wandering in the wilderness were required of God's people. Confederate soldiers read accounts that emphasized how Moses, Joshua, and other Old Testament heroes had triumphed over enemies such as the Amalekites. Outnumbered Confederates could exact similar triumphs. "What we have to do is to give ourselves to *prayer*," urged one soldier. In this way, historian Kurt Berends has argued, "Writers ensured the readers did not miss the parallels between Israel and the Confederacy. In the annals of history, both nations served Divine purposes."[12]

Southerners compared figures such as Stonewall Jackson to Moses, bolstered by the lore that quickly grew up around stories of his stern Old Testament faith and his accidental death at the Battle of Chancellorsville. His end was a "dark dispensation" that should serve as a "stern reproof for our idolatrous regard for man," warned one minister. Attorney general of Virginia John Randolph Tucker used similar imagery. As he saw it, Jackson, like Moses, foresaw independence for his people but died (literally) in the Wilderness and "resigned his mighty soul to heaven."[13] The Old Testament accounts helped to explain defeat as well, for they told of God's chosen people being led into captivity, "but that fact did not prove the heathen to be right in the cause nor that the Israelites were upholding a bad cause."[14]

If spirituals gave voice to an enslaved people, the southern proslavery and prowar sermon fulfilled a similar incantatory function for whites during the war. Also akin to the spirituals, Moses and Jesus (and their respective supporting casts) appeared in abundance. Each of the narratives helped white southerners wrestle with the meaning of wandering, war, violence, defeat, and redemption.

Just as whites identified with Moses and the children of Israel more than is commonly understood, black slaves fastened onto the biblical character of Jesus in ways that scholars have understated. Scholar and theologian Allen Callahan recently has described the Bible as a "Talking Book" for African Americans. The Bible, he argues, constituted at once a "poison book" full of the scriptures of enslavement and a Talking Book containing the antidote to its own poison. Some of that antidote was Jesus, who appears alongside Moses in the literature, song, and oral narratives of African American Christians in the eighteenth and nineteenth centuries. As a black minister in Virginia told a congregation, "I have come to say my last word to you. It is this: none but Christ." The suggestion that the highlighting of Jesus in twentieth-century African American gospel songs contrasts with the spirituals of the nineteenth century ignores the abundant evidence of Jesus as a central figure in African American religious expression even before the Civil War (as explored in more detail in chapter 3 of this book).[15]

More than that, the spirituals exalted more obscure Old Testament heroes as well as Moses, and often turned New Testament figures such as Jesus into avenging heroes. These biblical heroes, moreover, were immediately available, for the slaves' sacred world invoked a kind of constant present. Sacred time merged with real time.

Moses *and* Jesus thus populated the slaves' spiritual universe. If the spirituals identify with the story of Moses, they ring with affirmations of Jesus as well. "Steal Away to Jesus," the slaves sang; "Steal away, steal away home / I ain't got long to stay here." With its obvious connotation of stealing oneself away from the slave master into freedom, this spiritual serves as a primary exhibit for those who interpret the sorrow songs as coded messages of freedom. But such distinctions of temporal and spiritual were foreign to the world of slaves. Thus, to decode the "real" meaning of any spiritual leads away from richer understandings of their multiple levels of meaning.

If Moses was more a part of white southern sacrality than is commonly understood, then the same may be said for Jesus as a central figure in antebellum black religious expression. The two figures intermingled through songs, sermons, and stories. Their mythological arcs informed theological discussion and everyday religious practice. In the 1810s, a black woman named in the records only as "Aunt Katy" attended a North Carolina Methodist gathering. In the midst of a revival service, she felt the spirit and "with many extravagant gestures, cried out that she was 'young King Jesus.'" Black worshippers knew that she was filled with the spirit; she was channeling the voices of the ancestors through the language of Jesus. The presiding white minister, Joseph Travis, drew a different lesson from his encounter with the enthusiastic congregant; she was deluded and had to be read out of the congregation. Travis reflected positively on his own action, writing later that his discipline had rendered the eventually penitent woman as a "rational and consistent member of the church."[16] This slave woman's direct identification with Jesus, along with a white presiding authority who dismissed the initial explanation of her encounter, set a pattern for the covert and overt meanings of black Christianity in the slave South. Jesus captured

Aunt Katy's spirit in ways derived directly from African conceptions of soul transformations.[17]

Wherever travelers went in the nineteenth-century South, they heard songs of Jesus, often from the voices of the disenfranchised: women and slaves. Moses was there too, of course, and more slyly tricksters and conjurers, but as one spiritual expressed it, "Everywhere I go . . . Somebody's talking about Jesus." Stories of him suffused the evangelical South. He often materialized in a blaze of bright glory or riding a milk-white horse. "If you want to find Jesus, go in the wilderness," went one slave spiritual. Although illiterate, a freedwoman in Beaufort, South Carolina, said she could "read Jesus in my heart, just as you read him in the book. . . . I read and read him here in my heart just as you read him in the Bible. O . . . my God! I got him! I hold him here all the time. He stay with me." A slave woman with swollen limbs followed the voice of Jesus in healing herself by putting beaten peach-tree leaves over her limbs, which alleviated her suffering. "Doctor Jesus tells me what to do," she later recalled.[18]

Jesus's humble birth, miraculous deeds, gruesome execution, and glorious resurrection often came to slaves through the words of white ministers and missionaries. Soon enough they could be found everywhere in the black southern imagination, often retold and re-envisioned in ways that freely mixed biblical characters from different time periods. Slaves encountered Jesus when they retreated to the woods seeking conversion experiences, in times of extreme turmoil, during whippings and beatings, and in their own dreams and visions. A young slave in South Carolina in 1850 saw Jesus in heaven, "a sittin' behind de door an' a reading his Bible." In moments of transfiguration, slaves observed the physical presence of God or Christ. One said, "I looked away to the east and saw Jesus. . . . I saw God sitting in a big arm chair." Another saw him "when he freed my soul from hell"; still another related his encounter with Jesus in a "snow-white train" moving as quick as lightning, Jesus on board as the conductor.[19]

Black Christians related finely grained details of Christ visions, down to the parting of his hair in the center. They often perceived

God as white. As one expressed it, "I saw the Lord in the east part of the world, and he looked like a white man. His hair was parted in the middle, and he looked like he had been dipped in the snow, and he was talking to me." Another said, "Then Jesus came to me just as white as dripping snow, with his hair parted in the middle just as white as snow." Candidates for conversion were robed in white. They saw themselves carried on white chariots and white horses. In visions, the converts themselves became white. "The first time I ever saw a vision," recounted one ex-slave, "I saw myself a little body, pure white, and flying along a beautiful stream that flowed from the east." After a conversion experience, another ex-slave remembered, "the next morning everything was white. My hands were like snow. They just shined. They looked like the sun was on them."[20] Slaves spoke of a "little me" inside a "big me," and Jesus often appeared as a "little" or "small" man, a gentle guide to the soul represented by the little me.

Jesus's saving power could break the shackles of the dungeon and cleanse the soul. Repeatedly, the metaphor of cleansing, of making the soul whiter and purer, appears:

> Remember the day, I remember it well
> My dungeon shook and my chain fell off
> Jesus cleaned and made me white
> Said go in peace and sin no more
> Glory to God, let your faith be strong
> Lord, it won't be long before I'll be gone.[21]

Later, black theologians worried over the frequent invocations of whiteness, and black artists deliberately portrayed black Christs in poetry and painting (this is discussed further in chapter 3). In the nineteenth century, images of Jesus as a white European flowed from religious publishing houses and flooded the nation, giving many Americans their first experience with mass-produced images of Jesus. In part, the descriptions of Jesus provided by slaves and ex-slaves remembering their conversion experiences must have come from these ubiquitous prints. In the colonial era, Jesus had no appearance, and no race; by the mid-nineteenth century, he had become a white man. Yet, for many slaves, whiteness seems to have been more symbolic of purity and salvation rather than literally denoting a color, and it in no way hindered identification with a Jesus whose white imagery belied his black sympathies.[22]

Slave visions reinforced the sense of seeing, feeling, and being with a variety of biblical characters, especially King Jesus. Black Christians placed the crucifixion, resurrection, and triumph of Jesus in the present tense; exodus and salvation were part of the same process. Jesus could have come like a king in resplendent glory, a slave minister told his congregation. But "did he come only to the rich? . . . No! Blessed be the Lord! He came to the poor! He came to us, and for our sakes!" Theologian Allen Callahan expresses it this way: "African Americans read their own collective experience into the agony and exaltation of Jesus. The story of the Christ child, blessed by God yet both in the shadow of poverty and violence, was their story. Jesus's humble birth in antiquity signified the humble origins of African peoples in modernity. In his impoverished entry into the world, Jesus turned the tables on earthly valuations."[23]

Spirituals and other slave songs told of Jesus in his multiple roles. He was a conqueror and a mighty warrior, as in this compilation of verses about "King Jesus":

> Ride on, King Jesus
> No man can a-hinder me
> Ride on King Jesus, ride on
> No man can a-hinder me
> I was young when I begun
> No man can a-hinder me
> But now my race is almost run
> No man can a-hinder me
>
> King Jesus rides on a milk white horse
> No man can a-hinder me
> The river Jordan he did cross
> No man can a-hinder me

> If you want to find a way to God
> No man can a-hinder me
> The gospel highway must be trod
> No man can a-hinder me
> When I get to Heaven gonna wear a robe
> No man can a-hinder me
> Gonna see King Jesus sittin' on the throne
> No man can a-hinder me
> Gonna walk over those streets of gold
> No man can a-hinder me
> Goin' to a land where I'll never grow old

In many other settings, Jesus was a friend and comforter:

> Well, I been travelin' all through this way
> Well I take Jesus, he will be my friend
> Well, I been travelin' through this way
> Well, I cried out
> I take Jesus to be my friend
> He will lead me, safely through
> Whiles I'm travelin', whiles I'm stumblin' all the time.
> When I'm on my lonesome journey, I want Jesus Be with me.

Many spoke of just being in the presence of Jesus:

> I'm going to sit down by my Jesus
> O yes, I'm going to sit down by my Jesus, some of these days, hallelujah
> I'm going to sit down by my Jesus
> I'm going to sit down by my Jesus
> I'm going to sit down by my Jesus, some of these days.

Jesus would come to the rescue of the suffering people in Egypt:

> Jesus Christ, He died for me
> Way down in Egypt land
> Jesus Christ, He set me free
> Way down in Egypt land

Moses, Jesus, Absalom, and Trickster

Jesus and Moses were linked to the fate of Israel and captive people everywhere. "By stationing Jesus back with Moses," theologian Dwight Hopkins explains, "the entire Exodus event becomes a paradigmatic foreshadowing of the liberation consequences of Jesus' death and resurrection—the universal poor's grand exodus from poverty to freedom. The slaves were radically centered on Jesus."[24]

Slaves placed the crucifixion, resurrection, and triumph of Jesus in the present tense: "Dey nail Him to de cross . . . Dey rivet His feet . . . Dey hanged him high . . . Dey stretch Him wide." King Jesus rode as a warrior on a milk-white horse with sword and shield. "Ride on, King Jesus," slaves sang. "Ride on, conquering King," for "the God I serve is a man of war."[25]

The biblical heroes of Moses and Jesus populated the religious imagination of both whites and blacks in the South. Wandering in the wilderness, experiencing crucifixion, suffering alongside Jesus, and then perceiving a resurrection to come—the biblical stories spoke to the experiences of blacks and whites through the trauma of slavery, the Civil War, and postwar recovery. When examining the spread of evangelicalism in the South, it would be easy enough to stop there. The paradigmatic Old and New Testament stories of Moses and Jesus seem to sum up the most fundamental message that pervaded evangelical sermons, songs, literature, and private imaginings.

And yet: the southern Christian stories of Moses and Jesus ultimately were not capacious enough to speak to the full range of human experiences and relationships. Enmeshed in a complex world of slavery and race, of human bondage and family intermingling, of hierarchical order and amoral chaos, of love and theft, southerners needed a deeper well of myths from which to draw. Other stories fulfilled this need. They came from music, myth, folktales, film, literature, art, and poetry.

Southern Tricksters

If Moses and Jesus represent the two dominant biblical personae of southern evangelical history, the mythopoetic figure of the

Trickster and the tragic son Absalom stand as two counter- and contra-themes. Moses and Jesus assured Christians of victory over suffering, of making it out of Egypt, forging a people, and gaining redemption from temporal captivity and spiritual bondage to sin. The Trickster and the story of Absalom, by contrast, suggest darker, more morally ambiguous stories. After brief definitions of "the Trickster" and of "Absalom," used here as archetypes and cultural personae rather than as direct referents, the remainder of this chapter will focus on examples from two primary categories: southern vernacular musical forms and William Faulkner's murky and magnificent novel *Absalom, Absalom!*, along with its black counterparts *Beloved* and *The Known World*.

Moses and Jesus powerfully blessed and emblematized in personal narrative the experiences of wandering, suffering, crying out to God, being delivered, and crossing to the other side in triumph. Moses signified endurance and deliverance; Jesus, unendurable and unjustified suffering, and ultimate triumph. The biblical figures stood as cultural paragons. But like all peoples, white and (most especially) black southerners struggled to comprehend mystery, evil, suffering, and death. They required a theodicy as well as a way to understand the moral ambiguities of life. They depicted Moses and Jesus in primary colors, as victors in a Manichean struggle of good and evil. They needed figures of grey, able to exist both in this world and in the underworld. Slaves, in particular, confronted an amoral world at odds with the apparent meaning of religious texts. They encountered power in the person of slave masters against which no figure, not even Moses or Jesus, could stand.

Ultimately, tricksters and Absalom figures were as necessary as Moses and Jesus. Moreover, folktales, mythologies, blue notes, country tricksters, and spirit possession were as integral to southern evangelical culture as theological treatises, hymns, baptisms, and belief in Jesus. A rich cultural tradition survived the smothering rhetoric of "uplift" pervading church organizations, and it later found its way into new church formations such as Pentecostalism. Magic, conjure, casting spells, exchanging or stealing lovers, divining intentions and riches, shape-shifting oneself into a new persona—all of these and more informed the countercultures that circled the edges of southern evangelicalism. Southerners readily borrowed from the morally ambiguous characters in stories about mythological tricksters, devils, and figures from the nether regions. Both European and African traditions, carried to North America, readily supplied such a cast of characters to serve such a purpose.

Observers at the time, and scholars since, have focused primarily on African and African American tricksters as seen in slave tales of Br'er Rabbit and others, as well as in folklore and blues songs. These tales implied that weaker characters could deploy sly wit and devious deceptions to overcome stronger forces. They also pictured an amoral world in which even the weapons of the weak could be turned inward on a community. Once the genie of deception materialized out of the bottle, then all could be an illusion. Animal characters sometimes tricked each other regardless of status; humans could do the same. As Lawrence Levine has explained, "the trickster served as agent of the world's irrationality and as reminder of man's fundamental helplessness. . . . If the strong are not to prevail over the weak, neither shall the weak dominate the strong. Their eternal and inconclusive battle served as proof that man is part of a larger order which he scarcely understands and certainly does not control."[26]

During slavery, conjure men personified tricking, with their array of both beneficial and malevolent formulas for root bags and other objects invested with supernatural power. Observers of antebellum black spiritual practice frequently commented on the presence of conjure, also called hoodoo or black magic. Whites (and some Christianized blacks) simply condemned it as superstition. Evidence for the prevalence of conjure may be found in the early colonial era, as when a Virginia Anglican commented on how slave fugitives placed "confidence in certain figures, and ugly Representations," desperately hoping these talismans would protect them from discovery. White missionaries provide much raw material for analysis of the slaves' ideas and perceptions, including the world of conjure. In the 1840s, Charles C. Jones, a large slave owner in the Georgia low country and the most prominent exponent of the mission to the slaves, noted that Georgia slaves believed in "second-sight, in apparitions, charms, witchcraft, and in a kind of Satanic influence." Patsy Moses remembered her grandfather telling her about "conjure and voodoo and luckcharms and signs," with "voodoo doctors" having "meetin' places in secret and a voodoo kettle and nobody know what am put in it, maybe snakes and spiders and human blood, no tellin' what. Folks all come in de dark of de moon, old doctor wave he arms and de folks crowd up close. Dem what in de voodoo strips to waist and commence to dance while de drum beats. Dey dances faster and faster and chant and pray till dey falls down in a heap." Slave Christianity and African American folklore were intermixed. A white observer in the 1860s "found among the religious slaves of the South traces, more or less distinct, of a blending of superstition and fetichism, modifying their impressions of Christianity." Hoodoo and conjuring, a postbellum observer commented, was "very probably a relic of African days." Those defined outside the realm of civil society thus invoked "secret and supernatural powers" to seek justice or vengeance. After the Civil War, another observer found that ministers and congregants talked "freely at their religious gatherings of 'tricking' and 'conjuring' and tell marvelous tales of the power of those endowed with supernatural gifts." Or, as a conjure woman named Seven Sisters put it, "It's a spirit in me that tells—a spirit from the Lord Jesus Christ.... I tricks in the name o' the Lord." Such conjurers later achieved immortal fame in J. T. "Funny Papa" Smith's blues tune "Seven Sister Blues."[27]

Conjure and Christianity were in theory antithetical but in practice complementary. Studies of the mutual relationship between magic and religion show how informally envisioned and formally wrought worlds of the supernatural interact, collide, complement, and supplement one another. The practice of conjure, a form of healing and counterharming that drew from both Christian and African-based religious elements, was the province of poor southern blacks who were its primary practitioners (although whites formed a substantial clientele base). Fears of unseen powers compelled frequent recourse to conjure men. Belief in supernatural powers wielded by especially gifted men and women—or at least a willingness to suspend disbelief—pervaded much of the Deep South. Many southern believers, black and white, engaged in a Pascalian wager, trusting in their Christianity but also keeping one foot in the world of spirits invoked by conjurers and narrated in popular tales. It was self-evident wisdom to place some stock in both. Deeply held notions that imparted spiritual meanings to objects in the natural world remained a resilient part of southern folk understandings. Anthropologist Hortense Powdermaker, for example, found numerous ministers in Mississippi in the 1940s who doubled as "Voodoo doctors," and she realized that "those who are devoutly religious are also devout believers in current folk superstitions," for they did not see religion and conjure as "conflicting in any way."[28]

Slaves in need of special powers to heal, harm, love, or trick commonly consulted conjure men. These folk priests claimed special powers and knowledge of the spiritual potentials of natural materials. Black southerners often believed that children born with a caul covering their heads or with some other physical mark would become conjure men or otherwise evidence some special access to the spirit world. The masters of hoodoo assembled bags of natural or man-made materials that might contain roots, toad's feet, snake's teeth, the tails of rabbits, snail's shells, rusty nails, flannel, and human hair, fingernails, or toenails. The bags could be placed under the pillow of an enemy, who would then experience some calamity, or near the cabin of a person seeking protection. Whites in the backcountry South also sometimes consulted the conjure men, for European American folk beliefs contained much premodern lore paralleling that of Africans and African Americans. In an age of ineffective or even harmful professional medicine, ordinary Americans sought relief from illnesses and ailments wherever they could.[29]

During the years of the rise of evangelicalism and, eventually, the development of evangelical theology, religion and magic in time became categorized as separate spheres of knowledge. But for many southerners, white and black, they were not yet understood that way. Both involved ritual incantations and invocations of supernatural power. But the worlds of conjure and magic occupied a sphere of moral ambiguity, offering answers that evangelical religion could not, or would not, provide. For white and black religious reformers, Christianity and conjure were inherently contradictory. For many black southerners, they were complementary, addressing spiritual needs at different life moments. For enslaved people, conjure supplemented Christianity. They were two ways of accessing the spirit world. Conjure provided certain pragmatic benefits that Christianity did not. On the other side, Christianity provided reassurance about the fate of human souls in a way that the pragmatic manipulations of conjure could not address.

Beyond conjuring, religious figures, including Jesus, could act as tricksters, unsettling the social order with tales of overturning it. The African American religious imaginary conjured apocalyptic visions from biblical passages (as detailed further in the next chapter). In the early years of the Chesapeake and South Carolina, religious figures populated the southern imaginary in ways that suggested a merging of the powers of the Christian trinity with those of other nether regions.

The trickster appears occasionally in the spirituals. More frequently, he shows up in folktales and (especially in the twentieth century) in folk song, particularly country and the blues. In religious song, the trickster usually plays the role of devil, alternately seducing or frightening the listener. The devil/trickster as portrayed here bears a more striking resemblance to the conjuring trickster of West African folklore than to the unambiguously evil Satan of the Western Christian tradition. "The Devil's mad and I'm glad / He lost the soul he thought he had," one familiar chorus went. The Devil became "a liar and a conjurer" in many songs, a human-like figure who tricked and deceived humans rather than overpowering them with ineffable evil:

> Old Satan is a liar and a conjurer, too;
> If you don't mind, he'll conjer you.

Tricksters remained constant haunting, mocking presences, always there to unsettle and question human verities and to entice the curious into seductive worlds of pleasure. The world of sexual pleasure, forbidden in the church, constantly beckoned as an enticement, as in Blind Lemon Jefferson's tune "Low Down Mojo Blues": "My rider's got a Mojo, and she won't let me see / Everytime I start to loving, she ease that thing on me." While the partner "hid" her mojo, the singer knew he "got something for to find that mojo with." In signifying variations on lyrics about mojo powers and hands (which transformed African gris-gris and conjure-men root bags into symbols of male virility) and king snakes crawling, bluesmen embodied and played out the trickster visions of ambiguity, pleasure, and strange powers. In this sense, they were as quintessentially religious figures as the preachers, for in profoundly personal ways they explored the boundaries of the sacred and the profane. They "preached" the blues, and audiences shouted in response. In those cases, they served as preachers dispensing "secular spirituals." Many of them followed prodigal-son cycles in their own lives, going through the blues life and then finding redemption and giving up the blues to preach. The examples from the life stories of blues characters turned preachers are numerous and include many of the music's founding luminaries such as Son House, LeDell Johnson, J. B. Lenoir, Blind Willie McTell, Skip James, Gary Davis, Rubin Lacy, and Gatemouth Moore.[30]

Because blues singers' words spun tales of bad men and heroes (John Henry and Railroad Bill being two of the best known) who performed incredible acts and boasted of superhuman powers and sexual prowess, they personified the trickster. Bluesmen and blueswomen spun tales of selling their souls to the devil—most famously, Robert Johnson's tale of meeting the devil at the crossroads or Peetie Wheetstraw's boast of being the "devil's son-in-law"—but they may have done so, musicologist Jon Spencer speculates, precisely because they were not that frightened of the evil presence. Closer to the trickster gods of Africa than to the darkly powerful Satan of Western Christianity, the devil in African American folklore was a force at once attractive, amusing, and frightening, just as were the bluesmen themselves.

Preachers and bluesmen offered two seemingly contradictory but ultimately complementary versions of black spirituality. Providing neither the collective solace of spirituals nor the optimistic swing of gospel, the blues instead commented on the inability of humans to sustain relationships, improve their condition, or encounter the Sacred as something other than a trickster. The country blues sketched a collective wisdom that spoke truth to power but also reinforced social enmities among powerless people.

"The blues" as a character representing black suffering and the human condition often stands in as a trickster figure, as in the numerous versions of the blues represented as a person or apparition greeting one in the morning: "Good mornin', blues, / Blues how do you do," and "I was up this morning, blues walking like a man / worried blues, give me your right hand." Jon Spencer argues that this "personified blues" was "the personality of the African trickster-god and his African-American derivatives, which functioned as models of heroic action for those who fought for sustenance at the underside of history." In other cases, realities of farming life—rivers, mules, horses, the boll weevil, other insects and critters, plants containing natural remedies—taunt the limitations of humans. The great Mississippi River flood of 1927 inspired Charley Patton's classic "High Water Rising," in which the river shows its power over men unable to stop its force. And in one of many boll weevil tales, the insect defies a farmer who puts him in the hot sand by insisting that he'll "stand it like a man."[31]

White southerners inherited parallel, if not identical, traditions. They existed further underground and often appeared in the guise of Christian symbology. In a sense, they were "folklorized" earlier. That is, they were suppressed more effectively, written out of respectable intellectual dialogue or cultural practices earlier than the like characters of the African American heritage. Nonetheless, white folklore of strange sightings, tricksters, devilish imps, witches, and strange beings coursed through rural communities, sometimes traversing the color line, often fascinating white and black alike. "More than half of the white people" in Beaufort County, North Carolina, believed in "witches and jugglery," a school teacher there noted in 1867; such observations appeared frequently in writing about southern "superstition" during the era. William Wells Brown, the escaped slave turned author, found that whites were "possessed with a large share of the superstition" that was ubiquitous in the region, while a folklorist for the Hampton Institute found in Rockingham County, Virginia, an "astonishing" degree of belief in conjurers among whites, adding that it was "not confined to the lower class."[32]

White southern folk and country music, too, handed down exquisitely painful sagas about the supernatural forces that shaped everyday lives, sometimes inexplicably and often for the worse. For every "May the Circle Be Unbroken" that expressed evangelical aspirations to heaven, there were songs about the mysterious cuckoo bird warbling, bad luck befalling innocent souls, gambling debts piling up, ghosts and apparitions haunting communities at night, crimes of passion and rage tearing apart communities, and death stalking humans on the brink. The folksong "Coo Coo Bird," the jaunty hard-luck tune "Jack of Diamonds," and the plaintive classic "O Death," which features death as a character coming into the room and the singer pleading to "spare me over another year," all explored how unexplainable happenings affected human life. And tunes from the shape-note hymnals such as *Southern Harmony*, older folk ballads such as "Poor Wayfaring Stranger," and more recent variations on it such as "Rank Strangers," reinforced the idea that this was a "world of woe" in which "everyone I met / seemed to be a rank stranger." In heaven there would be only family, but on this world of woe there very well could be no one to actually know, much less trust.

White southerners, especially those of the upcountry and mountain regions, spun stories that sprang from Elizabethan English, Scottish, and Irish roots. They told of rough-and-tumble lives, unwelcome visitations by "hants" and "hags" (variations on the theme of the widespread belief in "witches and jugglery" that nineteenth-century observers noted), and murderous psychopaths whose deeds haunted communities for generations. In a contemporary version of this tale, Gillian Welch's "Caleb Meyer," the protagonist is a woman who survives a brutal sexual assault in her mountain cabin by plunging the glass from a broken bottle of whiskey into her assailant's neck, killing him. But the ghost of the assailant stalks her: "Caleb Meyer, your ghost is going to wear those rattlin' chains / But when I go to sleep at night, don't you call my name."[33] "Pretty Polly" and countless other murder ballads retold stories of homicidal rage directed against cheating lovers. Sexual infidelity, alcoholic benders, cheating at cards, and killings of rivals run through much of this music, where the characters seem unable to escape from predestined fates and from unseen forces controlling their behavior. Contemporary variations such as "Long Black Veil" have played with the tradition by portraying characters falsely accused of murder who cannot own up to the truth, even at the cost of their own lives: at the time of the murder, they were with their best friend's wife. Later, country musicians tamed and popularized these stories into formulaic but satisfying three-minute ballads and up-tempo honky-tonk tunes of drowning sorrows at the bar, seeking out love in all the wrong places, and explaining to perplexed city slickers that "country folk can survive."

Tricksters, apparitions, and bad men, then, came in various guises in white and black communities. They represented the portion of the southern spiritual world that could not be encompassed by heroic biblical figures. It was not a pretty world, nor one that could be saved, and yet expressing it artistically was as necessary as preaching the evangelical world to others. Whites found ways, as did African Americans, to Christianize tricksters, not because they could be tamed or domesticated, but so that morally ambiguous characters could be incorporated into a broader religious world view. In one case, country music great Hank Williams created his own persona, "Luke the Drifter," which gave him voice to articulate homespun religious sentiments very much at odds with the boozing and womanizing reputation he developed (and to some degree deliberately cultivated) as a songwriter and performer. Inverting the usual pattern, Williams's trickster was himself, while his stage character Luke dispensed bromides of religious wisdom that he never managed to follow in his own short and troubled life.

Sometimes, the trickster and Jesus could merge into a powerful figure. For African Americans especially, as historian Edward J. Blum has expressed it, Jesus could be a trickster of the trinity. Blum writes, "At first, African Americans who described Jesus used the language of lightness and brightness. It was not until into the nineteenth century that whiteness became the defining feature of visions of Christ. But even then, African Americans saw a distinct Jesus—one that whites could hear about but whom they would never understand. The white Jesus became the trickster of the trinity, able to enter the world of whiteness, defy it, and sometimes dismantle it."[34]

Jesus as trickster profoundly unsettled the social order. He roamed the land in white southern nightmares of murder and mayhem and induced the turn to a proslavery theology that, while profoundly powerful in its premises, was also deadly deluded. Slaves thus embraced a Jesus that the whites around them feared and tried to repress (as the following two chapters will explore in more detail), for Jesus's own life and message were a trickster tale of how the powerless might overcome the powerful through parable and poetry.

Absalom in Southern Literature

The final theme to be explored here comes from the biblical story of King David's son Absalom. After trying to avenge the rape of his sister by their half brother Amnon, Absalom leads a revolt against David's forces. As he rides into the climactic battle, Absalom catches his hair in the boughs of an oak tree and is left hanging. David's men discover him, and he is killed by his father's commanding general, Joab. The tale of incest, rape, and family intrigue in the story of Absalom from 2 Samuel has resounded with particular force in southern literature. Ultimately, if Moses and Jesus represented endurance and triumph and the Trickster insinuated himself into the cracks of the wall between good and evil, the figure of Absalom represents the southern entanglement with race and sex. His tale captures the drive to purity and the inevitability of hybridity in a society so dominated by the commingling of power and race.

David famously cried out "O Absalom, my son, my son." William Faulkner southernized the biblical tale in *Absalom, Absalom!*, a work exploring the confluence of unconscious incest and miscegenation in the Thomas Sutpen family of Yoknapatawpha County, Mississippi. The predetermined nature of the tragedy comes through in the title and also in the frequent comments of characters who understand themselves to be players in a drama whose ending is inevitable. As one character puts it, "Yes, fatality and curse on the South and on our family as though because some ancestor of ours had elected to establish his descent in a land primed for fatality and already cursed with it."[35]

Yet somehow out of that tragedy had come a civilization that had its moment of magnificence. The grace of southern social life arose from "a soil manured with black blood from 200 years of oppression and exploitation until it sprung with an incredible paradox of peaceful greenery and crimson flower" (202). The self-proclaimed "design" of the main character, Thomas Sutpen, is to live in the world of the great planters. He came to that realization while young, the child of poor whites in the mountains. While growing up, he did not realize there was any difference between white men beyond "lifting anvils or gouging eyes or how much whiskey you could drink then get up and walk out of the room" (183). Sent on an errand to deliver a message to the master in the "big house," he met a black butler at the door. The servant barred the young Sutpen from entering, telling him to go to the back, just as he would have told a slave. And then, "all of a sudden," Sutpen "discovered, not what he wanted to do but what he just had to do, had to do it whether he wanted to or not, because if he did not do it he knew that he could never live with himself for the rest of his life" (178). He understood that it was not "the nigger," who was "just another balloon face slick and distended with that mellow loud and terrible laughing so that he did not dare to burst it," but rather the big house owner who saw him and his kind "as cattle creatures heavy and without grace, brutely evacuated into a world without hope or purpose for them." (189). It wouldn't do to kill the messenger (the butler), he understood, because "to combat them you have to have what they have that made them do what he did. You got to have land and niggers and a fine house to combat them with" (192). This realization sends Sutpen on his journey to create a world where he would never be bossed and humiliated again. The pursuit of that "design" foreordains his tragedy.

Sutpen's long backstory comes to us late in the novel, after his downfall and desperate attempt to recreate his life following the Civil War. He tells the narrator of his poor upbringing, his sojourn in Haiti and creation of a plantation world there, and later his move to New Orleans and then to Mississippi, where he shows up as a stranger whose history is completely unknown. To the local populace of Faulkner's fictional county, Sutpen appears as a "demon." Seemingly out of nowhere, he materializes "suddenly ... with two pistols and twenty subsidiary demons." He wrests lands from local Indians and on his plot of one hundred acres builds a mansion even before making a plantation. He hires a French architect to design the big house; when that architect flees, Sutpen employs his slaves and his dogs to track him down, just as he would do with a fugitive slave. To stuff the big house, he went away with six wagons and "came back with the crystal tapestries and the Wedgwood chairs to furnish it and nobody knew if he had robbed another steamboat or had just dug up a little more of the old loot" (145). He succeeds in building up his plantation and acquiring a wife from the shopkeeper Goodhue Coldfield's family. Evangelicalism and Honor meet in Coldfield and Sutpen, for Coldfield was a man who "owned neither land nor slaves except two house servants whom he had freed as soon as he got them, bought them, who neither drank nor hunted nor gambled" (14). That wife, Ellen Coldfield, bears him his son Henry and daughter Judith.

Henry is a product of Thomas Sutpen's "design" to carve a plantation out of the Mississippi wilderness and bequeath to his son his fortune. At the University of Mississippi, Henry befriends a sophisticated young classmate from New Orleans, Charles Bon. Unbeknownst to Henry, Charles is (we are led to assume) his half brother; worse, he is the son of Thomas's first wife, a woman who (as we gradually learn from tales spun from the imaginations of other characters) likely had some taint of African blood and thus could not fit in Thomas's design. The story unfolds when Charles appears at the University of Mississippi, befriends Henry, and then determines to marry Judith. The sophisticated Bon simply overwhelms the backwoods Sutpen family with his elegance and gentility. But Thomas Sutpen forbids the marriage, evidently having discerned Charles's identity. Charles is a "mistake" in the design, and his presence leaves Sutpen with a choice: "either I destroy my design with my own hand, which will happen if I am forced to play my last trump card, or do nothing, let matters take the course which I know they will take and see my design complete itself quite normally and naturally and successfully to the public eye, yet to my own in such fashion as to be a mockery and a betrayal of that little boy who approached that door fifty years ago and was turned away, for whose vindication the whole plan was conceived" (220). Sutpen's dilemma in pursuing his design or preserving family purity is the South's dilemma writ small.

Feeling loyalty to his beloved friend, Henry Sutpen leaves his father's house. Henry and Charles fight together with the University of Mississippi's student contingent in the Civil War. Slowly, gradually, and agonizingly, Henry queries Charles about his identity. Or so the scene is imagined by the main narrators of this part of the story, the young southerner Quentin Compson and his Canadian college roommate, Shreve, who conjure up and even *become* and channel Henry and Charles as they sit in a Harvard dorm room recreating what must have happened between the two. Henry, they come to believe, gradually understood why his father had forbidden the marriage to Judith, and Henry must likewise forbid it. Charles's being partly black in this retelling of the biblical story makes the rape of his half sister all the more horrible to her full brother, Henry. But as Charles taunts Henry (again, in the imaginative retelling of Quentin and Shreve), "So it's the miscegenation, not the incest, which you cant bear. Henry doesn't answer" (285). Henry can bear Judith's marrying her half brother, but he cannot bear her marrying a half brother who carries even an indistinguishable trace of African blood. When Charles pushes forward anyway, Henry murders him, flees, and disappears for forty years, returning only at the end of the novel when the narrator Quentin Compson and another townswoman discover him at the decayed Sutpen mansion, now a house permanently haunted by its past. The remaining servant of the Sutpen household, Clytemnestra (Clytie, the daughter of Sutpen by a slave woman), and Charles Bon's grandson from his previous marriage in New Orleans, a mentally handicapped man called Jim Bond, set fire to the decayed Sutpen mansion, completing the story and fulfilling all the necessary elements of the tragedy.

Earlier in the novel, Rosa Coldfield, the daughter of the town's sternly Methodist shopkeeper, has come out to Sutpen's Hundred upon hearing of Charles Bon's death. Like others in the Sutpen household, the puritanical Rosa had fallen in love with Charles—or, more specifically, with the idea of grace and hedonism that Charles represented. Charles lies dead in an upstairs bedroom. Rosa demands to see him but is stopped by Clytie, who touches her on the arm and tells her that she may not go upstairs. Although as much Sutpen as black, Clytie embodies a black presence in the novel more than Bon, "the abstraction who is made 'nigger' in order to complete the pattern of the legend."[36] The effect of Clytie's touch on Rosa's arm is electric: "Because there is something in the touch of flesh with flesh which abrogates, cuts sharp and straight across the devious channels of decorous ordering," Rosa later reflects. The contact of human flesh across even an unseen color line could destroy an entire social order that seemed so solid and yet was so fragile: "Let flesh touch with flesh, and watch the fall of all the eggshell shibboleth of caste and color too" (112). With these words, Faulkner takes a story focused on a son's rebellious act and murderous rage and turns it into a tale of sexual impurity, incest, and most importantly, miscegenation and racial impurity.

Absalom, Absalom! explores the American myths of innocence, success, righteousness, and victory, juxtaposed with the southern experience of pain, evil, struggle, and defeat. Faulkner's words call to mind C. Vann Woodward's analysis in "The Search for Southern Identity": "The experience of evil and the experience of tragedy are parts of the Southern heritage that are as difficult to reconcile with the American legend of innocence and social felicity as the experience of poverty and defeat are to reconcile with the legends of abundance and success."[37]

Sutpen's trouble, Faulkner makes clear through the voice of one of his narrators, is "innocence." The contrast here between innocence and corruption is stark. His design is simple, and it is the design of the men who scrabbled their way up to become the planter class. But it is a design deeply invested in the least innocent and most violent of human institutions. Sutpen's inability to acknowledge it comes in his interpretation of the trouble with Charles Bon—it would constitute a "mistake." Either Charles would destroy the household and the design, or he would have his marriage to Judith and the design would then become a giant fiction, with generations of Sutpens being fatally tainted from the start. Sutpen could not allow it, and neither could Henry.

After returning from the Civil War, his son Henry now vanished and Charles dead, Sutpen attempts to start over. He first proposes marriage to Rosa Coldfield, the younger sister of his deceased wife, Ellen, but will only formalize their marriage after Rosa bears him a son. The grimly prim Rosa spends the rest of her life in vengeful retellings of her version of the Sutpen story. Sutpen then moves on to the daughter of his hired hand, Wash Jones, but insults her too, inciting Jones eventually to kill Sutpen. An illiterate poor white man, Jones represents the person Sutpen was originally, and he ponders the same mysteries of innocence and class in the South that originally had set Sutpen off on his journey. Wash wonders about the world "where niggers, that the Bible said had been created and cursed by God to be brute and vassal to all men of white skin, were better found and housed and even clothed than he and his granddaughter—that this world where he walked always in mocking and jeering echoes of nigger laughter, was just a dream and an illusion" (226).

Sutpen's story must be written into the southern arts, precisely because it could not be told within the confines of southern evangelicalism. For southern evangelicals had become part of the very false innocence, as had Thomas Sutpen, once they had accepted the design of slavery. Moreover, the spread of Sutpen's design coincided with the explosion of evangelicalism through the antebellum era. Once that design had spread from being concentrated on the eastern seaboard to its eventual home through all of the states of the slave belt, then southern evangelicalism became part of a family tragedy that its theology could never fully comprehend. Thus, stories from the Bible, particularly the Old Testament, had to be exploited in song, poetry, and literature, for only there could the full tragedy of race, miscegenation, and "impurity" in southern history be told. As literary scholar Eric Sundquist explains,

> The heroic stature of Sutpen and his willed "innocence" are no more denied by his sons than are David's by Absalom and Amnon; and in the biblical account, David's cry—the novel's title—is prompted not by Absalom's murder of Amnon, who has raped their sister, but by the later death of Absalom, the son who has risen up in rebellion against his father. It might well have been Lincoln's cry, and it might, seventy-five years later, have been Faulkner's. Like the fall of David's house, the fall of the South seemed more and more to Faulkner, in myth and in fact, an extended fulfillment of prophecy or, more exactly, a lasting curse for original sins.[38]

Faulkner plays deeply with the black image in the white mind, the ways in which whites projected onto blacks their own complex of fears and dreads. He does this in part through the voice of Rosa Coldfield, who categorizes Sutpen himself as one of the "demons" who had touched flesh in ferocious wrestling matches with his band of "wild niggers" early in the novel, told as part of Sutpen's wresting a plantation and a mansion from a Mississippi wilderness. Sutpen's hand-to-hand combat with his band of "wild niggers" establishes his masculine authority within the system of southern honor. But Rosa, the daughter of the Methodist shopkeeper who refused to fight in the Civil War, could only see Sutpen's actions as stemming from the same self-degradation that later led him to propose breeding with her, and marrying if that experiment were successful. And Faulkner also plays with projections of blackness in part through Sutpen's recognition that the "monkey niggers" he saw in his visions were not real; they were abstractions of a larger class system that he sought to crack by becoming a master himself.

Finally, the power of the image in Faulkner's novel comes through the characters' retelling of the relationship of Thomas Sutpen, his son Henry, and his (likely) son Charles Bon. None of the surrounding characters knows the full story, and the reader has to piece it together through the repeated (and often inaccurate or speculative) retellings. By the end, the college-student narrators have placed themselves in the position of Henry Sutpen and Charles Bon; they enact imagined conversations they believe could have happened between the two, playing up their belief that Charles used his black blood to taunt Henry. No one can know what happened between Charles and Henry or Henry's motivation for murdering Charles after forsaking his plantation birthright by running away with him. The story can be known only through its being passed down, traded, speculated on, invented, and reinvented with each telling. And with the retellings, the speculations about the meaning of Charles's tainting of Sutpen's design, his contaminating it with his black blood, become more prominent, until at the climactic scene—again invented in the minds of Quentin and Shreve—Charles taunts Henry with his inability to tolerate miscegenation. Later, as Quentin and Shreve come to understand the tale, Henry feels compelled to murder Charles, acting in some ways as a surrogate for his father and also protecting the purity of his sister. None of this can be known for certain by the reader, just as it was not known by the characters enacting the tragedy. The speculation and innuendo build until an intolerable and explosive climax, both for the characters involved and for those who, a generation later, are retelling the events and speculating about them. The novel concludes with Shreve's posing a shattering question to Quentin, whose response foreshadows his own suicide, a month later in time and described in the novel *The Sound and the Fury*. Commenting on the entirety of the Sutpen story, Shreve sarcastically opines that

> "in time the Jim Bonds are going to conquer the western hemisphere . . . and so in a few thousand years, I who regard you will also have sprung from the loins of African kings. Now I want you to tell me just one thing more. Why do you hate the South?"

"I dont hate it," Quentin said, quickly, at once, immediately, "I dont hate it," he said. *I don't hate it* he thought, panting in the cold air, the iron New England dark: *I don't. I don't! I don't hate it! I don't hate it!* (303)

Toni Morrison's master's thesis concerned Faulkner, and her best-known novel, *Beloved*, takes on Faulknerian themes, except told through the words of women and their children. In *Beloved*, Morrison took her inspiration from the story of Margaret Garner, a real-life slave woman in Kentucky who had borne children probably fathered by a relative of her former master. After Garner and her husband and family escaped across the Ohio River to an area near Cincinnati, they eventually were caught in a safe house, where Garner murdered one of her young daughters and prepared to kill her other children before being apprehended. Garner's owner transported her back to slavery in Kentucky, and he avoided allowing her to be extradited back to Ohio, where she would be tried as a free person rather than as property under the Fugitive Slave Law of 1850. A year later, having been sold to new masters first in New Orleans and then again in Mississippi, she passed away from typhoid fever in 1858.[39]

In *Beloved*, Morrison fictionally extends the story into the post–Civil War era, allowing readers to experience the post-traumatic ordeal of slavery through the personal torment of Sethe, the main character, as projected onto the lost child. "I got a tree on my back and a haint on my house" (18), Sethe says. The "tree" is the root and branches of scars from beatings she took as a slave. The "haint" [haunt, or ghost] in her house is the child she murdered rather than seeing her subjected to slavery. Morrison transforms the Absalom tale into a female story of slavery's horror. The necessity of killing one's offspring, and the haunting presence of that act afterward, dominates the novel. Beloved, the child-ghost come to life, is a trickster who will haunt and suck the life out of Sethe.[40]

In Morrison's fictionalized world, Sethe and other slaves in the Garners' Kentucky household have planned to run away to escape their new owner, a character named Schoolteacher, who stands in for the worst form of scientific racism and phrenology (the nineteenth-century pseudoscience of measuring skulls as an alleged test of human racial intelligence). Schoolteacher is obsessed with measuring and quantifying his human stock for his own sadistic purposes. Sethe's mother-in-law, Baby Suggs, resides just across the river in Cincinnati, where she serves as an informal exhorter of the kind represented in real life by Jarena Lee and other black female traveling evangelists of the early nineteenth century. Sethe has sent her children ahead to stay with Baby Suggs while she and the other slaves of the Garner household plot their escape. A band of men from the Garner household nabs the pregnant Sethe just before she is ready to flee, and then suck from her breasts the milk that she is storing for her young children in freedom and for the child that will soon be born. Watching this act is Sethe's husband Halle, who is reduced afterward to enacting his own impotence by slathering his face with butter from a churn. Driven insane by watching Sethe's rape, Halle disappears from Sethe's life, never following her to freedom and, in Sethe's eyes, abandoning the family.

In her horror, Sethe flees, stumbling toward the Ohio River in a scene that deliberately reenacts the story of the runaway female slave Eliza from *Uncle Tom's Cabin*. Along the way Sethe meets a poor white girl, Amy Denver. Amy helps Sethe deliver her new child, and Sethe names the child Denver in Amy's honor. Sethe makes her way to Cincinnati and to her mother-in-law's house. The family celebrates her escape but overdoes it in the eyes of the locals. The "scent of their disapproval lay heavy in the air," and the townsfolk "whispered to each other in the yards about fat rats, doom and uncalled-for pride" (162). The locals fail to warn the family of Schoolteacher's appearance with three others, described in the novel as the "four horsemen" and by Beloved as "the men without skin." The slave catchers have come to wrest Sethe and her family back across the river.

Seeing the four horsemen of her apocalypse, Sethe plans to kill all her children, but manages only to saw through the neck of one of the children she originally had sent ahead to safety across the river, the girl who later reappears as Beloved, or at least so the characters in the novel believe. Sethe's act horrifies even the brutal slave catchers, who now cannot take her back. Judged insane, she is moved to a house that becomes the setting for the novel. Sethe's murdered child haunts that house and eventually drives away Sethe's new male love, Paul D, and Sethe's youngest daughter, Denver.

As the novel progresses, the ghost-child Beloved increasingly dominates the house, throwing around the adult man Paul D at will, torturing her sister Denver by monopolizing their mother Sethe's attention, and frightening neighbors who fear getting anywhere near the haunted house. Beloved as a character shows the continuing haunting presence of the memory—or, as it is called in the novel, the "rememory"—of slavery, and the tale serves as a mournful reminder of how an Absalom tale would play out for a mother of the antebellum black South. Further, in this version of the tale, the child's vengeful acting out occurs after death, as a "haint," rather than in a willful rebellion in this life, a choice unavailable to slaves.

Morrison's revisiting of the tale of fratricide has fewer direct biblical parallels than some of her other novels (such as *Song of Solomon*), and the Absalom story, one based on father-son conflict, is not a direct inspiration. Yet Morrison's insightful readings of Faulkner's tales, including *Absalom, Absalom!*, suggest her regendering the story. This regendering makes the story the more awful because it involves the unconceivable: a mother killing her own child. And through this reworking of the story, Morrison enters into several southern literary traditions at once: the gothic, the Absalom story, and the slave narrative.

Also like *Absalom, Absalom!*, Morrison's novel is structured as a series of reminiscences about a particular story. With each retelling, the narrative grows deeper and darker, and with each retelling individual characters provide their own perspectives on a complicated tale that cannot fully be grasped by any one person. Early in the novel, Sethe recalls the price of her journey. "I got a tree on my back and a haint in my house, and nothing in between but the daughter I am holding in my arms," she tells Paul D. "No more running—from nothing. I will never run from another thing on this earth. I took one journey and I paid for the ticket, but let me tell you something, Paul D Garner: It cost too much! Do you hear me? It cost too much" (18). The novel begins near the end of the tale, in 1873, by which point Sethe, her daughter Denver, and Beloved, the mysterious girl who appeared from nowhere and whom the others believe to be the ghost of the murdered baby, reside at a house enumerated by its address, "124." Townspeople avoid them, considering the house haunted, and Beloved, a character with seemingly supernatural powers, has come to take possession of Sethe. "Stooping to shake the damper, or snapping sticks for kinlin, Sethe was licked, tasted, eaten by Beloved's eyes. Like a familiar, she hovered" (68).

Sethe's girl born en route to freedom, Denver, has come to understand the connection between Sethe and the lost daughter Beloved: "Sethe was trying to make up for the handsaw; Beloved was making her pay for it. But there would never be an end to that, and seeing her mother diminished shamed and infuriated her." Diminished and infantilized as she was by Beloved, Sethe feared Beloved's leaving before Sethe could make her understand "what it took to drag the teeth of that saw under the little chin; to feel the baby blood pump like oil in her hands; to hold her face so her head would stay on; to squeeze her so she could absorb, still, the death spasms that shot through that adored body, plump and sweet with life" (295). Yet Beloved's presence is killing her mother, as Beloved figuratively eats her alive with her obsessive demands for attention, her control of the house, and her ability to repel others from entering.

Baby Suggs, Sethe's mother-in-law, has made her name with her open-hearted preaching: "She did not tell them to clean up their lives or to go and sin no more. She did not tell them they were the blessed of the earth, its inheriting meek or its glorybound pure. She told them that the only grace they could have was the grace they could imagine" (103). But later, Baby Suggs resigns herself to the fact that she has lied while "124 shut down and put up with the venom of its ghost." Suggs ran an open house, full of townsfolk coming by to share in her blessings. But Sethe, Beloved, and Denver's residence meant "No more lamp all night long, or neighbors dropping by. No low conversation after supper. . . . There was no grace—imaginary or real—and no sunlit dance in a Clearing could change that." Baby Suggs's heart had begun to "collapse" after Sethe arrived (105).

Stamp Paid, one of the other slaves from Sweet Home, the Garner home in Kentucky, seeks to make Baby Suggs preach again. He accuses Suggs of blaming God and giving in to the fact that the "whitefolks won." The conversation continues with Suggs's reply:

> [Baby Suggs]: "I'm saying they came in my yard."
> [Stamp Paid]: "You saying nothing counts."
> "I'm saying they came in my yard."
> "Sethe's the one did it."
> "And if she hadn't."
> "You saying God give up? Nothing left for us but pour out our own blood."
> "I'm saying they came in my yard."
> "You punishing Him, ain't you."
> "Not like He punish me."

Later, Stamp Paid realizes that Suggs was right: "they came in her yard anyway, and she could not approve or condemn Sethe's rough choice. One or the other might have saved her, but beaten up by the claims of both, she went to bed" (211–12). Earlier in the novel, Suggs has insisted to Sethe that she "lay down her sword and shield," lay down all of it, just relinquish the burden she has been carrying. But on this point, too, Suggs concedes. The reason to lay down the sword and shield is that "this wasn't a battle, it was a rout" (244).

In *Beloved*, Morrison builds on the meanings of whiteness as it came to be expressed in its binary, in blackness. In white mythology (as explored also in *Absalom, Absalom!*), under every black was a jungle "ready for their sweet white blood," and "the more coloredpeople spent their strength trying to convince them how gentle they were, how clever and loving, how human, the more they used themselves up to persuade whites of something Negroes believed could not be questioned, the deeper and more tangled the jungle grew inside. But it wasn't the jungle blacks brought with them to this place. . . . It was the jungle whitefolks planted in them.

And it grew. It spread. In, through and after life, it spread, until it invaded the whites who had made it. Touched them every one. Changed and altered them. Made them bloody, silly, worse than even they wanted to be, so scared were they of the jungle they had made. . . . the red gums were their own" (234). These were the red gums that sneered out at Henry Sutpen from behind Charles Bon's falsely aristocratic face and demeanor. This projection of blackness was a fear of barbarism all the more powerful because of its allure and because it could go unseen in a person.

A final reworking and reenvisioning of the Absalom tradition in southern literature comes in Edward P. Jones's *The Known World*, published in 2003. In this novel, Jones tells the story of black slave master Henry Townsend, the son of Augustus Townsend, a furniture maker and slave to William Robbins. Henry's father has purchased his freedom, and Henry has become a protégé of Robbins and an expert boot maker. Seeking to make his way in his known world, Henry sets out to become a slaveholder himself, egged on by Robbins, a slaveholder whose primary love is not his wife but his slave mistress Philomena, with whom he has two children. From Robbins, Henry purchases his first slave, Moses, a linchpin in the novel.

> Moses was the first slave Henry Townsend had bought: $325 and a bill of sale from William Robbins, a white man. It took Moses more than two weeks to come to understand that someone wasn't fiddling with him and that indeed a black man, two shades darker than himself, owned him and any shadow he made. Sleeping in a cabin beside Henry in the first weeks after the sale, Moses had thought that it was already a strange world that made him a slave to a white man, but God had indeed set it twirling and twisting every which way when he put black people to owning their own kind. Was God even up there attending to business anymore?[41]

Henry's decision to become a master baffles his father, Augustus Townsend, who had warned him to stay away from whites and the whole slaveholding regime: "Don't go back to Egypt after God done took you outa there" (137). Augustus had sworn never to let a slaveholder set foot on his land but "never once thought that the first slaveowner I would tell to leave my place would be my own child." In his anger, Augustus takes a stick and beats Henry severely across the shoulder, knocking him to the ground. Henry stands up, breaks the stick in two, and responds coldly to his father, "Thas how a master feels" before riding off to see his mentor, Robbins. Augustus's former owner tells him to take everything he can get in this life, land and slaves and all, even if it has to be behind God's back.

Throughout *The Known World*, the characters ruminate on the parallels between their conditions and stories and those of biblical characters. One concludes, "The God of that Bible, being who he was, never gave a slave a good day without wanting something big in return" (337). At the beginning of the novel, Henry's wife, Caldonia, is keeping vigil over him as he slowly passes away. She and a free black woman who had taught Henry and others to read sit discussing a poem by Thomas Gray. Henry awakes, believing he knows which poem they are talking about. Then, just as he "formed some words to join the conversation, death stepped into the room and came to him: Henry walked up the steps into the tiniest of houses, knowing with each step that he did not own it, that he was only renting" (10–11). In death as in life, he is only renting his own status. Henry's father knows this much more bitterly. Through dint of his work and artisanal skill, Augustus Townsend has managed to free himself and his wife. One day, though, captured by some poor white and Cherokee patrollers who threaten to kidnap and sell him, Augustus retorts by showing them his free papers. One of the slave catchers takes the papers and eats them, reminding Augustus that his status is only as good as they decide it is. They seize Augustus and sell him back into slavery.

When he dies at the age of thirty-one, Henry has accumulated over thirty slaves and has run a plantation that appears to be another fulfillment of Sutpen's design. But like Sutpen's, Henry's design cannot withstand the forces of history. After Henry's death, Caldonia ineffectively tries to manage the family affairs, but she has neither the will nor the capability to do so. As the plantation deteriorates, Henry's slaves run away. His first slave, Moses, becomes

Caldonia's lover and yearns to become her husband but is thwarted when Caldonia marries a bastard son of William Robbins. Later in the novel, Moses's attempt to escape the Townsend plantation results in his capture; for his punishment, his Achilles tendon is cut, immobilizing him for life. By the end of the novel, Moses sits alone in a cabin, eating dirt, never having found his way out of his wilderness, much less to a promised land.

The story of *The Known World* depends in large measure on the illusions of the master class bequeathed to Henry, who as a black slave master is enmeshed in the same system of human property and must fulfill his role in that system. Henry "had always said that he wanted to be a better master than any white man he had ever known," but what he did not understand was that the "kind of world he wanted to create was doomed before he had even spoken the first syllable of the word *master*" (64). Like Thomas Sutpen's, Henry Townsend's design was doomed from the outset, and the elegiac novel traces his origins, rise, and eventual downfall much as *Absalom, Absalom!* does Sutpen's.

The parallels between Thomas Sutpen and Henry Townsend, and between Faulkner's saga of a white plantation's rise and fall and Jones's of a black plantation's, continue when William Robbins finds Henry wrestling with Moses on Henry's first day as a master, "like some common nigger in from the field after a hard day." Robbins wonders how anyone, "white or not white," could "think that he could hold onto his land and servants and his future if he thought himself no higher than what he owned. The gods, the changeable gods, hated a man with so much, but they hated more a man who did not appreciate how high they had pulled him up from the dust" (126). Henry's fighting may be compared with Sutpen's, too. At the end of an evening at the Sutpen household, members of the plantation gathered to watch Sutpen and a slave "both naked to the waist and gouging at one another's eyes as if their skins should not only have been the same color but should have been covered with fur ... a matter of sheer deadly forethought toward the retention of supremacy, domination" (*Absalom!*, 21). Henry, the black slave master, has even more need for that form of domination and wrestles Moses and other slaves in scenes directly reminiscent of the action in *Absalom, Absalom!*

The Absalom tale here is more allusive and indirect than it is in Faulkner, but the allegory nonetheless plays itself out in its basic structure. Henry is a wayward son who betrays his father in the deepest ways. His father has to expel him, as he does when he says, in pain, that he never thought the first slave owner he would have to run off from his house would be his own son. Augustus attacks Henry, physically breaking his shoulder but metaphorically killing him, or at least killing their bond. Henry joins the enemy forces, at first with apparent success, but that rising costs him his life at an early age, and the family he had assembled around him crumbles with him—as it must.

Conclusion: The Eggshell Shibboleth of Color

What do we learn from this brief tour through the uses of symbolism derived from Moses, Jesus, Absalom, and the Trickster? When we focus on evangelicalism in the South, we enter a complex world in which human hopes, dreams, desires, hatreds, and social organizations required a full range of symbolic sacred figures from the past for their full expression. Southern religious expressions often have been reduced to a tug-of-war between white versus black, Calvinist versus Arminian, Christian shame-based versus secular honor-bound, or evangelical piety versus guilty rowdiness. When we incorporate figures from the netherworld, from literature and poetry, from folktales and everyday speech, and from music and dance, we learn what religion in its broadest sense meant to people who lived in a region tortured by intractable social conflicts. It was not just the Puritan and the hedonist that writers from H. L. Mencken to Wilbur J. Cash have limned. It was the world in which Sutpen's design induced Sethe's unspoken suffering over her infanticide and Henry Townsend's rage at his own impotence even as a slave master.

White and black alike drew from the powerful narratives of Moses and Jesus, and both loved culturally variant versions of tricksters who queried, undercut, and mocked the social order on which evangelicalism depended. Their complex and mixed relationship found poetic form in the Faulknerian version of Absalom and his descendants in African American literature and song. Ultimately, they were so impossibly entangled that it was as if the Trickster ensured that the southern design for purity would be transformed into the southern reality of a biologically and culturally miscegenated region. When flesh touched with flesh, and when religious traditions commingled, what Faulkner called the "eggshell shibboleth of caste and color" would collapse.

CHAPTER TWO

"Because I Was a Master"

Religion, Race, and Southern Ideas of Freedom

Charles Colcock Jones, a Presbyterian planter and minister in the low country of Georgia, scorned slavery when younger but eventually emerged as the most effective advocate for the mission to the slaves in the 1830s. His complex relations with his large family and his slaves emerge in memorable detail and sensitive prose in Erskine Clarke's *Dwelling Place,* a beautiful work of southern history that shows how the insidious evil of slavery undermined the determined efforts of even the best-hearted people to redeem it. Jones saw his task as one of bringing light to those who came from pagan lands but could receive spiritual teachings about Jesus. Such instruction would have useful benefits for planters as well. Authority and obedience to masters would not be "felt and performed," Jones added, "*unless we can bottom it on religious principle.*" Knowledge of Jesus would redeem the evils that naturally arose from the condition of slavery. Jones articulated his life's mission in his 1842 work *The Religious Instruction of the Negroes in the United States.*[1]

Preaching before a slave congregation in 1833, Jones delivered a message about order and obedience from the book of Philemon. "When I insisted upon fidelity and obedience as Christian virtues in servants and upon the authority of Paul," he later wrote, and "condemned the practice of *running away,* one half of my audience deliberately rose up and walked off with themselves, and those that remained looked anything but satisfied, either with the preacher or his doctrine. After dismission, there was no small stir among them; some solemnly declared 'that there was no such ... Epistle in the Bible'; others, 'that they did not care if they ever heard me preach again!'" Some objected to his preaching "because I was a *master*."[2]

Charles Colcock Jones's experience suggests one of the deep paradoxes of American religious history: the explosion of democratic evangelicalism in the nineteenth century together with the rise of a racially repressive regime that grew from and depended on order, obedience, and hierarchy. The paradox played out in particularly powerful ways in the South. Thus, in writing a social history of religious ideas of freedom, there is no better place to start than the South. Such an exploration shows the ways in which freedom depended on un-freedom and how religious democracy, racial slavery, and social repression were intertwined.

The founding fathers personally held widely varying religious beliefs, from bare-bones assumptions about a generic "Providence" to more pious Christianity, but they largely agreed on abolishing established churches or religious tests for federal office. They were nearly alone in the western world in imagining a political order so disconnected from established religious institutions. Founders such as Thomas Jefferson believed that this would lead to a society based on rationalism rather than (as Jefferson saw them) biblical myths and religious superstitions. Contrary to those dreams, pietist religion deeply shaped American society in the nineteenth century; its influence was deeply pervasive and cultural, rather than strictly political. With the rise of the Second Great Awakening in the early nineteenth century, evangelicalism grew into a dominant form of religious expression. Toleration and religious freedom were the prerequisites for that growth. Yet the dominance of a particular form of Protestantism made religious freedom something of a myth. Nineteenth-century Protestants constructed a "moral establishment" that enforced, sometimes in law and other times in practice, a particular vision of order.[3]

Virginians such as Thomas Jefferson and James Madison, in league with evangelicals (especially Baptists) in the region, enshrined remarkably advanced ideas of religious liberty first in the founding documents of individual states and then in the United States Constitution. In this sense, the revolutionary-era South could claim to be at the forefront of individual religious liberty. In the nineteenth century, the spread of evangelicalism through the South suggested that religious liberties for individuals enhanced the religious growth of Christian denominations.

At the same time, Anglo-Americans throughout the country, but even more so in the South, created a racially exclusivist and religiously restrictive culture that limited the freedom, both civil and religious, of those defined outside the ranks of the free and the citizen. Southern evangelicals pressed for religious freedom. Yet they also repressed religious ideas of freedom that challenged their notions of order, and they extended a reign of bondage that made a mockery of evangelical ideals of equality. American—and southern—religious history fundamentally has been about this dialectic of religious freedom in the dominant nation, the racialization of peoples, and the resulting struggle to formulate alternative ideas of freedom and autonomy.

The religious diversity present from the early years of the North American colonies, the First Amendment, and the increasing pluralization of American society in the nineteenth century all created a context of official (if very partial) religious freedom and unofficial competition between religious groups. In some respects, Anglo-Americans fostered an intense religious democracy built on a foundation of American republicanism that assumed a close correlation between Protestantism and democracy. This world has been cogently described and celebrated in works such as Nathan Hatch's *The Democratization of American Christianity* and Mark Noll's *America's God*. At the same time, however, many evangelical religious ideas gave divine sanction to racial and social hierarchies, and formed the basis of proslavery thought in the nineteenth century.[4]

As a religious culture (as opposed to a legal polity), Anglo-American Protestantism was both liberating and hegemonic. Anglo-American Christianity in the early Republic spawned myriad groups that competed for souls. At the same time, European American Christian traditions conjured up a mytho-religious framework that racialized (that is, defined peoples into ever-evolving racial categories), and thereby subjugated, peoples.

Southern religious history centrally illustrates the broader story of American religious history: the powerfully and intensely paradoxical interplay of religious freedom/equality and religiously sanctioned un-freedom/inequality. In this dialectic, embattled ethno-religious communities deployed the American tradition of religious liberty as well as their own spiritual practices and sacred writings to compel redefinitions of freedom, autonomy, and the rights of citizenship. The discourse of American freedom thus undermined the ends envisioned by the Anglo-Protestants who authored the classic texts on religious freedom. Ethno-religious communal sacred narratives—such as the spirituals, the black counterliterature biblically refuting white supremacist thought, and later, the sacred songs and narratives woven into the civil rights movement—all redefined freedom by resisting and counterbalancing the dominant social, theological, and racial hierarchies.

This chapter explores the paradox of religious ideas of freedom and racial repression in southern history through three major narrative points. First, an examination of the encounter of African Americans with Christianity in the seventeenth and eighteenth centuries exemplifies many of the major themes that would characterize that relationship through the entire period of slavery—the suspicion of white planters about the meaning of Christianity for slaves and the creative adaptation of biblical texts by slaves who sought meaning and purpose in religious ideas intended to place them more firmly in bondage. Second, this chapter explores religious ideas of freedom and equality as they developed during the First and Second Great Awakenings, from the mid-eighteenth to the early nineteenth century. Finally, in looking at the contrast between the biblical exposition outlined in the proslavery argument and the spiritual moral narrated in slave spirituals and narratives, the chapter examines the context in which religious democracy and evangelical repression defined the contradictory soul of Christianity in the South. The next chapter, focusing more particularly on the figure of Jesus, follows this story to the civil rights movement, when the black counternarrative emerged victorious and the white supremacist story was driven underground into a folk theology of segregation.

Rebellions, Revivals, Revolution

Early colonizers in the Americas faced first the question of whether Christianity would apply to black slaves at all. The answer required, in part, deciding whether Africans and African Americans were fully human—a debate that raged for several centuries, into the post–Civil War era of scientific racism. If only Christians were truly men—and Christians were white—then where did that leave Negroes? English and Anglo-American theologians grappled with the problem. Was there a separate category apart from "man" into which blackness could be fit? As one early commentator put it, Negroes were "a people of beastly living, without a God, lawe, religion, or commonwealth." Heathenism thus was inextricable from barbarism and blackness, from being a not-Christian. In 1699, the Virginia House of Burgesses noted that "the negroes born in this country are generally baptized and brought up in the Christian religion; but for negroes imported hither, the gross bestiality and rudeness of their manners, the variety and strangeness of their languages, and the weakness and shallowness of their minds, render it in a manner impossible to make any progress in their conversion." Africans were, moreover, "accustomed to the pagan rites and idolatries of their own country," as expressed by a missionary for the Society for the Propagation of the Gospel in Foreign Parts. Ten years later, in 1724, an Anglican parish leader found that slaves had "so little Docility in them that they scarce ever become capable of Instruction." No wonder that English Christians seemed indifferent to Christian duty: "most men are well satisfied without the least thoughts of using their authority and endeavors to promote the good of the souls of those poor wretches," one critic exclaimed.[5]

Before the Great Awakening, the indifference and resistance of masters together with the prevalence of African religions and Islam meant that Protestant Christianity was a relative rarity among slaves. Whether slavery and Christianity were even compatible—

not to mention whether enslaved people possessed souls as whites did—were open questions for debate. White settlers remained unconvinced whether blackness ultimately was compatible with the state of being Christian. For many, blackness conjured images of savagery even in the practice of religion itself. The Reverend Morgan Godwyn, who ministered in seventeenth-century Virginia, charged that "nothing is more barbarous and contrary to Christianity, than their . . . Idolatrous Dances, and Revels." Other early day Anglo-American commentators found no clear biblical explanation for black skin color but nevertheless assumed it must signify inferiority. "We must wholly refer it to God's peculiar will and ordinance," wrote one Englishmen, invoking exactly the same evasion generally employed to "explain" why a good God allowed evil and unjustified suffering.[6]

As some slaves converted to Christianity, however, reality once again mugged ideology and theology. Anglo-Americans wondered if baptism would require freedom; that is, did baptism into the Christian religion make men *white*? The answers to these questions contained momentous implications for American ideas of freedom. The early advocates of slave Christianization accordingly dissociated Christianity from whiteness—from freedom—precisely for the purpose of defining "blackness" as a state of perpetual servitude continuing beyond one's potential baptism into the Christian faith and, indeed, beyond one's own life into the lives of one's descendants.[7] In 1664, the Maryland legislature worked out a law "obliging negroes to serve durante vita . . . for the prevencion of the damage Masters of such Slaves must susteyne by such Slaves pretending to be Christ[e]ned." In 1667, Virginians made clear the meaning of baptism for slaves:

> Whereas some doubts have risen whether children that are slaves by birth, and by the charity and piety of their owners made partakers of the blessed sacrament of baptisme, should by virtue of their baptisms be made free; *It is enacted and declared by this grand assembly, and the authority thereof,* that the conferring of baptisme doth not alter the condition of the person as to his bondage or freedome; that

diverse masters, freedom from this doubt, may more carefully endeavour the propagation of Christianity by permitting children, though slaves, or those of greater growth if capable to be admitted to the sacrament.[8]

Virginia's laws provided a model for later legislation.

The Glorious Revolution of 1688 further cemented the Protestant identity of Englishmen in the Old and New Worlds and the necessity of protecting true religion from dissenters and heathen Negroes and Indians. In the Chesapeake, that mostly meant Quakers and nonwhite people. One planter informed a Quaker bringing slaves to church to "restreyne his said Negroes & whole family from repairing to the said unlawfull Assemblyes at his peril."[9] The English defined their own Protestant identity further by differentiating it from the inalienable status of heathen. It was part of the larger project of defining freedom by enumerating what constituted the status of unfreedom. Virginia's 1705 Law of Servants and Slaves reinforced the legally enforced physical distinctions between Christians and heathens. The law stated that "all servants imported and brought into this country . . . who were not Christians in their native country . . . before they were shipped . . . shall be accounted and be slaves, and as such be here bought and sold notwithstanding a conversion to Christianity afterwards." The act forbade blacks and mulattoes from owning Christian servants "except for those of their own complexion."[10]

Before the Great Awakening, only a small trickle of planters found baptizing slaves of interest or even acceptable. Others struggled with convincing planters that Christianity was compatible with slavery. One preacher in 1710 made it his business "to represent the Groundlessness" of the view that slaves would be free after baptism, "plainly declaring that as far as I can apprehend, baptism makes no great alteration as to the outward circumstances of their slaves in this world, that it is merely out of Compassion and Charity to these poor creatures that we are so forward and earnest in teaching them" Christianity. He told the planters that they could expect better service from Christianized slaves "because whilst they continue ignorant heathens, they can expect at best but an eye service from them and such a obedience as proceeds purely from fear, whereas were they sufficiently instructed in the doctrine of Christianity, that would in all probability teach them obedience to their masters out of a Principle of Conscience and render them much more true and faithful to their interests than now they can reasonably be expected to be."[11]

For many Christians, whiteness simply became woven into the very fabric of Christianity, regardless of the laws about baptism. A Swedish traveler in the North American colonies noted how masters feared that Christianity would incite feelings of freedom and equality among slaves: "There are even some, who would be very ill pleased at, and would by all means hinder their negroes from being instructed in the doctrines of Christianity; to this they are partly led by the conceit of its being shameful, to have a spiritual brother or sister among so despicable a people; partly by thinking that they should not be able to keep their negroes so meanly afterwards; and partly through fear of the negroes growing too proud, on seeing themselves upon a level with their masters in religious matters."[12]

Over the coming decades of the evangelical revolution, planter resistance to slave conversion lessened in the face of the rise of the proselytizing power of the evangelicals. This suggests that slave owners came to see a Christian obligation, that African American converts pressed for recognition of their Christianity within the Church of England, and that rising generations of white southerners were more willing to support creole slave Christians whose parents had been baptized or had baptized their own children.

Still, the ambiguity of slave Christianization remained troubling. Christianity and whiteness were both states of freedom, making it easy for many to essentially equate the two: white equaled free and Christian; black/Indian/other equaled unfree and unchristian. Would not the ultimate freedom promised by Christianity infect the minds of the not-free, such that they would begin to question their status or to doubt the validity of Christianity? Whites had some reason to complain about restless Christian servants. Some slaves, particularly those of mixed race with some access to appealing to white authorities, were baptized into the Anglican Church and demanded that they be recognized as Christian men and women with rights. One plaintive plea from an anonymous group of mixed-race slaves arrived in the letter file of a newly installed bishop who oversaw Anglican affairs in the colonies. These slaves wrote that they were "Baptised and brouaht up in a way of the Christian faith and followes the wayes and Rulles of the chrch of England." They wrote to complain about the law "which keeps and makes them and there seed Slaves forever." The hardness of their masters kept them from following the Sabbath: "wee doo hardly know when it comes for our task mastrs are [as] hard with us as the Egyptians was with the Chilldann of Issarall." Their letter concluded with an explanation of why they did not sign their names, "for freare of our masters for if they knew that wee have Sent home to your honour wee Should goo neare to Swing upon the Gallass tree." These slaves retained an older, more radical view of Christian conversion: their religious status gave them rights to freedom and respect, for which they were willing to fight—in courtrooms, in letters to imperial officials, and as a last resort, in rebellions.[13]

It was difficult for many white Christians to feel secure in the extension of Christian freedom beyond the boundaries of Anglo-American society. This ambivalence, together with a cultural style of Anglican missionaries alien to African conceptions of religious practice, hindered the work of groups such as the Society for the Propagation of the Gospel in Foreign Parts (SPG).

Francis Le Jau, an early Anglican missionary with the SPG, faced a challenging task in his program of preaching to and Christianizing black slaves and Indians. He worked in South Carolina's Goose Creek Parish in the early eighteenth century, setting aside one day a week for the instruction of "Children, Servants, and Slaves" and, later, a class for slaves required by their owners to attend church.[14] Le Jau rebutted the widespread view among his parishioners that religious instruction would make slaves "proud and Undutifull." He contended that Christianity would produce more obedient and diligent workers, soon a standard justification among advocates of missions to slaves. "Many Masters can't be persuaded that Negroes and Indians are otherwise than Beasts," he noted in 1709, "and use them like such. I endeavour to let them know better things . . . but not all to my great Sorrow, on the Contrary what I do out of Charity is not well received. I wou'd think my self guilty of their own sins if I shou'd wink at things evidently evil." Moreover, as he saw it, dissenters, freethinkers, and those who prized Mammon above morality infected the colony. He declared the "plain truths" and avoided "Controverted tenets" but complained that "We are infected with Railers, Scoffers, & Atheistical persons, and those pretend to be the mighty Statesmen; God keeps us from seeing the World govern'd by their principles." Any minister who showed "zeal for Propagating Christian Knowledge and the Reformation of Manners," he realized, would uncover an "abundance of Enemies."[15]

Le Jau also feared the real possibility that slaves might feign conversion to achieve freedom, and he took measures to prevent such a possibility. "To remove all pretence from the Adult Slaves I shall baptize of their being free upon that Account," he told the SPG, he required a declaration from slaves that they did not *"ask for the holy baptism out of any design to free yourself from the Duty and Obedience you owe to your Master while you live, but merely for the good of your Soul and to partake of the Graces and Blessings promised to the Members of the Church of Jesus Christ."*[16] These reassurances failed to assuage masters who would "malign and traduce" those who encouraged proselytizing among the slaves. The legislature, moreover, considered conversion to be a drag on profits, for Christian slaves required time away from work for instruction and worship, and this for slaves who might "gull and deceive their masters" by putting on an "air and appearance of religion." Hence the planters concluded that "it is not only a sensible loss to them, but likewise too much time and pains thrown away to no purpose." To make matters worse, as Le Jau wryly noted, the masters gave them "likewise strange ideas of Christianity from the scandalous lives they lead."[17]

Given how biblical stories could inspire ideas that ran contrary to what even the most careful missionaries (such as Le Jau) taught, it certainly made sense for whites to fear that ideas of freedom would be transmitted in Christian language. Moreover, many in the colony were skeptical of whether blacks and Indians could be said to possess souls. Le Jau noted that "I cannot to this day prevail upon some to make a difference between Slaves and free Indians, and Beasts." One woman "considerable enough in any other respect but in that of sound knowledge" asked if it was possible that "any of my slaves could go to Heaven, & must I see them there?" Another young man swore he would not take communion with slaves. It simply constituted a violation of the social order. In 1712, Le Jau recorded his desire to baptize some more slaves who had been "well Instructed" and had no complaints concerning their conduct, but he noted that "Their Masters Seem very much Averse to my Design, Some of them will not give them Leave to come to Church to learn how to Pray to God and to Serve him, I cannot find any reason for this New Opposition but the Old pretext that Baptism makes the Slaves proud and Undutifull." Planters held on to this resistance even when Le Jau pointed out examples of slaves who had been baptized and whose conduct afterward was exemplary.[18]

Early southern evangelicals confronted the trickster Jesus in ways that made them profoundly uncomfortable. In the unstable world of eighteenth-century Anglican hierarchy and slave society, the evangelical Christian story incited social disorder. Or so it seemed to the cultural elite of that era. Most white Christians felt uneasy, at best, about the extension of Christian freedom beyond the boundaries of Anglo-American society. In one instance after another, from the Christian calendar that informed the Stono Rebellion to the preachers and exhorters behind Gabriel's Rebellion of 1800 and (so it was reported) Denmark Vesey's plot of 1822, scriptural teachings inspired unruly thoughts in slave rebels. White southern evangelical missionaries consistently faced the quandary of how to proselytize among slaves given the objections raised by a suspicious planter class. They faced further difficulties in controlling the message of evangelicalism when slave converts introduced their own theological creativity into interpreting the word of God in ways that only furthered planter suspicions and distrust.

In preaching to and Christianizing black slaves and Indians, Francis Le Jau faced challenges from whites as well as from his presumed proselytes. Le Jau's prize convert was also his biggest problem. This slave, the best black Christian scholar in his parish, was a "very sober and honest Liver," though, he continued, this slave's "Learning was like to Create some Confusion among all the Negroes in this Country." From the Christian message, however, Le Jau's convert related a disturbing vision. The slave parishioner "had a Book wherein he read some description of the several judgmts. That Chastise Men because of their Sins in these latter days, that description made an Impression upon his Spirit, and he told his Master abruptly there wou'd be a dismal time and the Moon wou'd be turned into Blood, and there wou'd be dearth of darkness and went away." He told Le Jau he had "read so in a Book," and when he spoke of his vision to his master, "some Negroe overheard a part, and it was publickly blazed abroad that an Angel came and spake to the Man, he had seen a hand that gave him a Book, he had heard Voices, seen fires &c." This early convert left vague the meaning of his prophecy. Probably he did not have to elaborate, for listeners could extrapolate from the apocalyptic imagery. Drawing from this experience, Le Jau exercised discretion in teaching slaves to read, acknowledging that "it had been better if persons of a Melancholy Constitution or those that run into the Search after Curious matter had never seen a Book."[19]

Regardless of the missionaries' reassurances about how Christianity would improve docility, Christianity and freedom were too closely linked for comfort. In 1725, the Reverend Richard Ludlam told of the treacheries "by secret poisonings and bloody insurrection" of slaves who had been brought over to Christianity. This, too, discouraged planters from spreading Christianity, "lest as they allege they should make such an ill use of meeting to do their duty to God as to take the opportunity at such times of seizing and destroying their owners." He hoped that God would bless his efforts with ecclesiastical superiors who would help him find bishops "some means . . . whereby thousands may be happily brought over to the Christian faith that they may enjoy the benefits (in their masters plantations) of Christianity without endangering their own or their owners happiness." In the previous year, the Reverend Francis

Varnod also noted that a chief obstacle to slave Christianization remained the fear that slaves would gather on the Lord's day to "make insurrections." He discovered that "some of [the] negro-pagans have a notion of God and of a Devil, and dismal apprehensions of apparitions." These were the kinds of "apparitions" that Nat Turner claimed to see in the sky and on corn plants a century later, just before his 1831 slave revolt.[20]

Slaves looking toward Florida saw not apparitions but genuine offers of freedom from a Spanish colonial presence intent on harassing the English colonies just to the north. The Spanish imported slaves to Florida, where they deployed them as soldiers to defend Spanish claims and harass the British settlement of South Carolina. In 1693, the Spanish Crown offered freedom to all fugitives who converted to Catholicism and served the Spanish king's military. These promises were not always kept. Nonetheless, word of the Spanish offer turned Florida into a magnet for fugitive slaves from the Carolinas. Africans manned Fort Mose, a settlement near St. Augustine built in 1738 and led by an African soldier named Francisco Menendez. Catholic priests required the new black Floridians to be baptized anew and then to receive additional religious instruction. A Spanish official observed that the slaves wanted to be Christians but their English masters sought to prevent them from learning Catholic doctrine.[21]

By 1746, blacks constituted about a quarter of St. Augustine's population of 1500. These included Africans imported directly by the Spanish, as well as fugitives from Carolina and other English colonies. Catholic priests sanctified marriages among the slaves and fugitives and baptized children. Membership in the church and the militia created ties of connection for these Atlantic creoles, who served the Spanish crown in exchange for their freedom.

The consequences of the unrest among slaves in the English colonies soon were evident in colonies such as South Carolina and New York, where slave uprisings erupted in 1739 and 1741 respectively. These rebellions suggested the connections between the religions of African peoples, their conception of slavery in North America, and the potentially dangerous consequences of Christian conversion. In both uprisings, whites pointed to Christianized slaves who took the lead in the revolts, adding to English fears about the effect of Christian preaching among people who lacked freedom but desired liberation.

On the Sunday morning of September 9, 1739, a slave named Jemmy, originally from the Kingdom of Kongo, gathered a group of slaves near the Stono River in South Carolina. They may have been inspired by recent runaways who had made it to Spanish Florida. The very date of the rebellion may have held a specific religious meaning for Kongolese Catholic rebels, who believed September 8 to be the day of Nativity for the Virgin Mary. Kongolese Catholics assumed that Mary held protective power for those who venerated her. The slaves also may have known about the recent South Carolina law that weeks later would have required all English men to carry firearms to church on Sunday to prevent slave revolts. Beating the deadline, Jemmy's posse broke into a store, secured firearms, and killed twenty-one whites. The next morning they marched "in a Daring manner out of the Province, killing all they met and burning several Houses as they passed along the Road."[22] Many of the rebels were likely trying to flee to freedom and away from their Protestant oppressors. That afternoon, white patrols gathered and killed thirty of the rebels. Some of the slaves escaped and remained fugitives for years.

As with the case of the Anglican slaves who had petitioned for their freedom in 1723, the Stono rebels likely understood the connection between Christianity and freedom. They evidently considered themselves to be Catholic Christians from an independent political kingdom. Some of them may have known how to fight based on their military experience with militia orders in the Kongo kingdom. Like the English, they understood that violence sometimes was necessary to defend one's freedom and one's faith. The Anglican idea that propagating Christian belief would inculcate order and obedience into an otherwise unruly slave population had failed. But low church evangelicals would soon make the same argument, with much greater success.

The Great Awakening

The Great Awakening first arrived in the South in the mid-eighteenth century when the English Anglican George Whitefield came to Charleston on one of his several speaking tours. Initially, he was a critic of slavery; by the 1750s, he was happy to be a slaveholder himself. Even then, he preached his message for whites and blacks alike. His exhortations reached a small group of planters in the low country of South Carolina, who responded to his call to save the souls of their bondspeople. One of them, Hugh Bryan, had a powerful experience that led him to proclaim "sundry enthusiastic Prophecies of the Destruction of Charles Town and Deliverance of the Negroes from servitude." The South Carolina Assembly punished Bryan for his insurrectionary outburst, but his comeuppance did not settle the matter for angry planters. They worried that white evangelicals were filling the heads of slaves with "a Parcel of Cant-Phrases, Trances, Dreams, Visions, and Revelations and something still worse, and which Prudence forbids me to name," referring to Bryan's visions for the "Deliverance of the Negroes from servitude."[23]

To rebut these kinds of accusations, evangelical Awakeners reprised the familiar argument that the slaves' Christianization would ensure obedience and good order among the servants. A New Light minister, Samuel Davies, preached to blacks in Virginia in 1757. He reported to his benefactors that when the slaves found a few moments of leisure, they came to his house. Davies led them in preaching and singing, and some of the slaves stayed all night in his kitchen. Davies awoke at 2:00 or 3:00 a.m. to find that "a torrent of sacred harmony poured into my chamber, and carried my mind away to Heaven"; such singing lasted all night. Davies knew that the great majority of blacks in the Chesapeake remained non-Christians like their African forebears, but he took heart at his success when one African-born man addressed him, saying, "I am a poor slave, brought into a strange country, where I never expect to enjoy my liberty. While I lived in my own country, I knew nothing of that JESUS I have heard you speak so much about." The slave was now determined to learn of the Savior. The evangelicals' early success among these Virginia slaves inspired Davies to muse that some of the Christianized slaves "seem to have made a greater progress in experimental Religion than many sincere Christians of a fairer colour." Davies recognized the peculiar situation of preaching spiritual freedom to enslaved peoples: "Many of them," he wrote, "only seem to be, they know not what. They feel themselves uneasy in their *present* condition, and therefore desire *change*." Some slaves, he knew, recognized salvation as potential liberation; they "would be baptized in compliance with the Fashion, and that they may be upon an Equality with their Masters," a fact that left him as uneasy as he was exhilarated by their "pious thirst for Christian knowledge."

Such teaching, Davies also pointed out, could have good effects in terms of ensuring the safety of the white population. During the French and Indian War (1756–1763), Catholic and Indian enemies of the British Empire harassed Englishmen on the frontier. Making matters worse, Davies wrote, English settlers feared "Insurrection and Massacre" from the slaves living among them. Responding to this dangerous situation, Davies urged slaveholders to bring slaves under the restraints of the pacifying "Religion of JESUS," which would teach them proper behavior within their social role and ensure the safety of the English colonies fighting their external enemies.[24]

This argument was never fully persuasive. Regardless of the laws separating baptism from freedom, the political implications of conversion were never clear, hence the perpetual uneasiness of whites about the safety of slave conversion. White exponents of preaching to slaves faced an uphill battle in persuading planters to support substantial efforts to convert African Americans. Remarkably enough, over time they largely succeeded.

During the Great Awakening and especially through the later eighteenth century, evangelical revivalists welcomed black people into their midst. Slaves exposed to Christianity in this manner responded enthusiastically; the clear parallels between African customs of bodily expressiveness in religious ritual and the much-derided enthusiastic worship practices of the early Baptists and

Methodists created remarkable scenes of interracial religious transcendence. The parallels between Baptist and Methodist preaching and practice (including, among the Separate Baptists, crying, falling down, and lying paralyzed on the floor) and African belief systems and religious rituals are obvious.

Revivalists and black converts collectively created religious excitements that eventually transformed the nature of southern religion. For example, the Methodist minister Thomas Rankin, preaching in 1774, was struck by the "number of the black Africans who have stretched out their hands and hearts to God," and he called on his congregation to look and participate in their spiritual joy. When he did, "It seemed as if the very house shook with the mighty power and glory of Sinai's God. Many of the people were so overcome, that they were ready to faint and die under his almighty hand." Rankin himself experienced an "uncommon struggle in my breast" as he watched the reaction of his congregation, "almost the whole of them upon their knees," singing and crying out. Rankin himself came to oppose slavery, although that was far from the norm for Methodist itinerants.[25]

Thus, while many observers still found that slaves were "as great strangers to Christianity and as much under the influence of Pagan darkness, idolatry and superstition, as they were at their first arrival from Africa," as did one traveler in 1779, the period for intensive evangelical efforts to Christianize the slave community clearly had begun. These efforts scarcely touched the majority of slaves. Nonetheless, the effects of the movement were profound and far-reaching. They would be felt even further in the nineteenth century, when Christianization of slaves became part of the reigning proslavery orthodoxy among devout planters and when a liberationist Christianity energized ideas of freedom and liberty in the slave community.[26]

The dangerous implications of evangelical preaching, at least as whites perceived it, emerged in some of the advertisements for runaway slaves during that era. Advertisements for runaway slaves from the time warned of fugitives who were noted for "affecting religious conversation" or for claiming to be Baptist preachers or to be "fond of singing hymns, and exhorting his brethren of the Ethiopian tribe." In 1793, slave owner Thomas Jones advertised for his fugitive slave, Sam, in a Maryland newspaper. The runaway had been raised in a family of evangelical churchgoers, the ad suggested, and lived with them virtually as an equal. He had been engaged in "exhorting his fellow creatures of all colors in matters of religious duties." Sam joined other early black evangelicals in preaching a message of gospel equality. Some went further than that. During a planned slave rebellion in Richmond in 1800, a black preacher compared the cause of rebellious slaves to that of the Israelites. In the Bible, he reminded listeners, God had promised that a small number of believers could conquer a much larger number of enemies surrounding them. The slaves could do likewise, he implied.[27]

The writings of African Americans who converted as a result of the Great Awakening constitute some of the earliest black American literature. They served as a charter generation of black evangelicals who spread black Christianity through North America. John Marrant authored one of the most important of these narratives. His story exemplifies the power, and the complexities, of black conversion to Christianity during the revolutionary era.

Born free in New York in 1755, John Marrant moved to South Carolina while still young. There, he became an apprentice and musician and devoted himself to "pleasure and drinking in iniquity like water; a slave to every vice suited to my nature and to my years." In 1770, he came to Charleston, where he had heard that a "crazy man was hallooing" in town. This "crazy man" was the famous colonial evangelist George Whitefield, whose circuit of preaching tours through the colonies drew huge throngs. The young prankster Marrant intended to disrupt Whitefield's service by blowing his French horn. Instead, Marrant fell under the preacher's spell. The message hit with such force that Marrant recalled being literally struck down by Whitefield's words. As he lay on the ground, those words felt like swords being thrust into him. He remained there until Whitefield came and said to him, "JESUS CHRIST HAS GOT THEE AT LAST." For three days Marrant fasted and prayed for salvation and at last felt that the Lord had entered his soul and given him eternal freedom. A black loyalist during the American Revolution, he later ministered to a group of black émigrés in Nova Scotia, Canada. After his death in 1791, about 1,200 of his black parishioners emigrated to Sierra Leone in Africa, where they established a Christian presence and carried on his work.[28]

The coming of Protestant Christianity to African Americans such as Marrant was a seminal moment in black American history. When Christianity came, moreover, black Americans adapted, shaped, and changed it. African American Christianity developed within the severe limitations of the slave regime. Regardless of the rhetoric of Christian freedom and equality, there was an obvious power gulf between whites and blacks in bondage. Slaves simply could not "make" their own world. Slaveholders held the power. Yet the actions of slaves constrained the power of slaveholders. Some slaves adopted Christianity enthusiastically and used their faith to challenge the premises underlying the slave regime. Through their actions, and those of white slaveholders, a complicated relationship developed between white paternalism, religion, and slave resistance. That history culminated in the rebellion of Nat Turner (discussed later in this chapter), whose religiously inspired visions compelled his furious and murderous resistance to the prevailing order of the South.

The Great Awakenings of the eighteenth and nineteenth centuries effectively created popular evangelicalism as the dominant style of American religious expression. They also recruited a charter generation of African American Christians into the larger evangelical culture. In doing so, the awakenings reinforced the principles that spiritual freedom did not extend to temporal liberation and that religious expressiveness could be embraced but also could be repressed when it appeared threatening. Black Americans could be in, but not fully of, the world of evangelical America. Christianity itself, with its universal message, could invite in all those in a community, but Christian institutions and the American nation emerging in the late eighteenth century would make sharp divisions based on evolving but apparently solid notions of race.

Despite the biblical admonition that in Christ there was neither Jew nor Gentile, slave nor free, American evangelicalism reinforced and policed racial boundaries in American society. The Great Awakening, with its message of equality and its success at attracting white and black believers, produced an American-style evangelicalism that might have undermined the country's racial system. Ultimately, however, evangelicalism defined and undergirded that racial hierarchy by declaring that the existing American social order reflected the will of God and that God expected men and women to perform their duties within their given stations. The religiously tolerant republic, the racialized nation that increasingly defined itself as a white Protestant republic, the messianic and millenialist dreams that inspired the rise of a democratic culture, as well as the aggressive expansionism that displaced and enslaved peoples all came together in the nineteenth century. American ideas of religious freedom emerged in such a conflicted context.

Slavery, Christianity, and Religious Ideas of Freedom in the Antebellum Era

As evangelicalism spread into the South in the late eighteenth century, slavery became an issue among the Methodists, Baptists, and Presbyterians who came to populate the region—not least because of the number of black converts who attended churches with their masters or, in some cases, independently. Trouble also arose when a number of early evangelicals expressed opposition to, or at least ambivalence about, slavery. John Wesley, founder of Methodism, decried the institution of slavery, and a number of early evangelicals followed his lead. Yet evangelical leaders also knew that, if they were to spread the gospel message to all classes, they would be preaching to slave owners as well as to common whites. And if they were to form strong religious institutions, they would need the intellectual and financial resources of wealthy and educated whites. To gain this support, they would have to make the necessary theological adjustments.

In the revolutionary era of the Great Awakenings in the South, a brief moment of opportunity for a biracial religious order seemed to present itself. Whites and blacks in backcountry congregations worshipped together. They called each other by the respectful evangelical titles "brother" and "sister" and wept to each other's exhortations. Some white Baptist ministers in Virginia declared slavery a sin, freed their slaves, and advocated lifting restrictions on black men who wished to preach the gospel in public.

But this moment was fleeting, for whites quickly learned to accommodate slavery with their desire to spread evangelical churches. In 1784, the Methodist Episcopal Church (MEC) had passed a church law requiring emancipation of slaves by white church members. Just six months later, the Methodists suspended that edict, and they never enforced it. Further, in the 1790s and early 1800s, local Baptist associations raised a firestorm of complaints about antislavery statements made by fellow Baptists, countering them with proslavery statements of their own. One planter in 1807 complained to the governor of South Carolina that the state housed numerous religious "Enthusiasts" who preached "very dangerous Doctrines and excit[ed] in our black populations Sentiments that must lead to fatal results."[29] Most planters wanted nothing to do with a religion that suggested anything about equality between souls. Given these attacks, the antislavery sentiment expressed by some early southern Baptists and Methodists would not survive into the antebellum era. Churches depended on converting slaveholders, as well as ordinary white men and women who wanted to become slaveholders.

In the early nineteenth century, the Christianization of the planter class, the introduction of slavery in the interior of the new nation, and the adoption of an ideal of the planter patriarch as "Christian steward" increasingly fed into planter support for missionary work among the slaves. So did the lessening of the original evangelical antislavery impulse. In 1801, when a Methodist antislavery pamphleteer published his views, residents of Charleston torched all the copies they could find of the offending text and assaulted a Methodist minister. Just a few years later, in 1804, newly rewritten Methodist denominational rules exempted churchgoers in several southern states from ecclesiastical rules that discouraged slaveholding. Methodist leaders such as Francis Asbury determined that converting slaves, not freeing them, best ensured the spread of

Methodism into areas of the country experiencing explosive population growth. Over the course of the nineteenth century, the alliance between the ministerial establishment and the master class strengthened. Together they discouraged black independent religious expression, which threatened good order, but encouraged white-supervised religious instruction.

In the nineteenth century, as white authorities increasingly took control of the "mission to the slaves," they limited the opportunities afforded to African American ministers and churches. Evangelical doctrine taught spiritual brotherhood and equality, but evangelicals patterned their churches and institutions after the larger social hierarchy of white authority and black subordination. The spread of Christian churches among the bondspeople allowed African Americans places of communal gathering and fellowship, while it assured whites that slaves were being "civilized" and taught biblical notions of a proper social order.

Christian thought and practice existed in a complicated, dialectical relationship with antebellum southern ideas of freedom. For white evangelicals, Christian freedom involved strict control. The exercise of church discipline and the vigilant self-policing of thoughts and behavior are abundantly evident in antebellum diaries. This inevitably created tension with the competing southern ideal of manly honor, which required assertive self-display. As evangelicalism spread through the slave South, bringing in men and women who formed the middling as well as the planter classes, Christianity increasingly informed the ideology of the master class. It wove itself into the fabric of plantation communities and growing urban environments in the South. At the same time, subversive readings of the Bible and of Christianity spread through slave communities and periodically frightened white authorities enough that they monitored or prohibited black religious meetings.

In the antebellum era, as evangelicalism extended throughout the South, white slave owners often brought slaves to church with them. In some cases, especially in urban centers in the South such as Richmond and Charleston, black congregants constituted a majority in "white" churches. In other cases, blacks attended their own churches, provided that whites remained in a supervisory capacity. Since slaves could not own property, white trustees held church buildings and other property for slave churches and also participated in the selection of their pastors.

By the 1830s, and even more so by the Civil War, wealthy southern men and women filled the pews of the same incipient denominations whose forebears they had disdained as zealous ranters. As spired steeples replaced log churches and unlettered exhorters gave way (at least in cities) to gentleman theologians, southern clergymen propounded their own social vision of God, country, family, and slavery.

As evangelical culture took its place in southern life alongside the male culture of honor and high-church Anglicanism formerly dominant in the region, devout planters faced a dilemma. Into such a milieu came the mission to the slaves, led most prominently by Charles Colcock Jones, the Presbyterian minister and slave-owning planter from the Georgia low country. He urged upon a wary but increasingly devout planter class the need to spread the gospel to enslaved people. It was a difficult sell in a region that constantly surveiled black gatherings and feared the spread of the doctrines of equality and liberty. Planters worried that such proselytizing would open the way for "men from abroad to enter in and inculcate doctrines subversive of our interests and safety" and that "the Negroes will embrace seasons of religious worship for originating and executing plans of insubordination and villainy." Jones crafted his response carefully.

> Being brought here they were brought as *slaves*; in the providence of God we were constituted *masters*; superiors; and constituted their *guardians*. And all the laws in relation to them, civilly, socially, and religiously considered, were framed by ourselves. They thus were placed under our control, and not exclusively for our benefit but for theirs also.
>
> We could not overlook the fact that they were men; holding the same relations to God as ourselves—whose *religious interests* were certainly their *highest and best*, and that our *first* and *fundamental*

duty was to provide to the extent of our ability, for the perpetual security of those interests. Our relations to them and their relations to us, continue the same to the present hour, and the providence of God still binds upon us the great duty of imparting to them the Gospel of eternal life.

He told planters that religious instruction would instill subordination and teach respect and obedience. Slaves who submitted to their earthly rulers and heavenly master ensured their reward in another life. It was the standard line of Anglican missionaries in the eighteenth century, and in the antebellum era it took hold in evangelical orthodoxy.[30]

By the 1830s, attacking slavery in public was nearly impossible in the South, and southern divines were preparing a vigorous theological defense of the peculiar institution. Some of them argued that slavery was a necessary evil, foisted on the South by Yankee slavers in the colonial era and now a living emblem of man's sinful and fallen state. They suggested that slavery could not be abolished without bringing even greater evils (anarchy, sedition, or even race mixing) in its wake. Some theologians interpreted slavery as a kind of Christian way station, educating black converts in the faith so that, in future generations, they could carry the message back to their home continent, thus fulfilling biblical prophecy.

Others attempted to prove that slavery arose from God's curse on the Negro as a race. They constructed elaborate narratives based on Old Testament passages to proof-text their dubious thesis. Passages from the Old Testament, especially Genesis 9:18–27 (which outlined the curse on Canaan, son of Ham, who had originally espied Noah's naked drunkenness)—once exegeted properly—provided at least a start at a religio-mythical grounding for modern racial meanings. With roots in the medieval era, when its "curse" applied to other groups (including Jews), this passage defeated generations of theologians' efforts to downplay it. According to historian Winthrop Jordan, the curse on Canaan, son of Ham—with Ham as a figure considered to represent black people; Shem standing in variously sometimes for Indians, other times for Jews; and Japheth supposedly being the progenitor of white people—was revived as a mode of biblical interpretation during the modern age of exploration, from the sixteenth century forward. It persisted through centuries in spite of "incessant refutation," and was, according to Jordan, "probably sustained by a feeling that blackness could scarcely be anything but a curse and by the common need to confirm the facts of nature by specific reference to Scripture."[31]

The passage popped up repeatedly in biblical discussions. In a typical nineteenth-century explanation, John Fletcher, originally a northerner who became a slaveholder in Louisiana, summarized how the curse on Ham's son could account for and justify American slavery. Ham's descendants, he said, were Africans, while Shem and Japheth, who preserved racial purity, were "blessed" with white progeny. Those relations of Shem and Japheth who intermingled with the Canaanite descendants of Ham were the Amalekites, whom the Israelites "were particularly commanded to destroy from off the earth." In their grim fate could be seen the future of those who would amalgamate with Ham's progeny. God thus doomed Ham's offspring to lives of servitude to the superior racial descendants of Shem and Japheth and commanded those blessed with a white heritage to avoid contaminating themselves through intermixing.[32]

Respectable theologians generally skirted or denounced the son-of-Ham story. It smacked more of folklore than high theology, and its persistence was something of an embarrassment to gentleman clerics. The fable nevertheless deeply penetrated the consciousness of ordinary white southern Christians, as seen in the poor white Wash Jones's musings about the curse in Faulkner's *Absalom, Absalom!* The son-of-Ham thesis explained how black people could be free Christians and unfree slaves at the same time. But the curse on Ham was at best a shaky foundation for religio-racial mythologizing, for the passage invoked was simply too short, mysterious, and fable-like to bear up under the full weight of the interpretations imposed upon it. Once again, as would so often be the case, the Bible proved a powerful but troublingly unreliable guide in the formation of mytho-racial ideologies. The evidence to support racial theologies seemed to exist, if only in bits and pieces, but so was the evidence for the destruction of human-constructed racial hierarchies. The New Testament did say "neither slave nor free." Ultimately, there would be no getting around that, although certainly not for lack of trying.

In *Mind of the Master Class*, historians Eugene Genovese and Elizabeth Fox-Genovese assert that "To speak bluntly, the abolitionists did not make their case for slavery as sin—that is, as condemned in Scripture. The proslavery protagonists proved so strong in their appeal to Scripture as to make comprehensible the readiness with which southern whites satisfied themselves that God sanctioned slavery. To this day, the southern theologians' scriptural defense of slavery as a system of social relations—not black slavery, but slavery per se—has gone unanswered."[33] This is no longer quite true, for we do have an answer provided by evangelical historian Mark Noll. Noll has suggested that arguments about slavery were fatally flawed by the "large role that extrabiblical racial axioms" played in works allegedly drawn from the Bible alone. He explains: "Personal interest, as satirized by Harriet Beecher Stowe, was certainly a factor. Even more important was the unbiblical assumption that slavery could only mean black slavery." Or as Noll puts it elsewhere, the "theological crisis involving the Bible and slavery" had several components, including "an inability to act on biblical teaching about the full humanity of all people," and "a confusion about principles of interpretation between what was in the Bible and what was in the common sense of the culture."[34]

The evangelical synthesis of Christian republicanism and commonsense reasoning, Noll argues, broke apart on the shoals of slavery. At one level, the issue was relatively simple. If the Bible could be read clearly and commonsensically, the words of God flowing freely out of that inexhaustible well, then why were Bible-believing Americans on both sides so irreparably divided by the existence of the very visible and seemingly intractable institution of slavery? Devout believers in the South, moreover, could point to leading theologians of the region, well-respected both at home and elsewhere, who had constructed formidable intellectual defenses of chattel slavery based (or so they said) on *sola Scriptura*.

Abolitionists, by contrast, were compelled to read Scripture more freely and even to step outside of it. They offered "spirit of" rather than the more common "letter of" reasoning from biblical passages to defend their calls for the immediate, uncompensated, total end to the enslavement of African-American people. Leading abolitionists such as William Lloyd Garrison, in fact, denounced the portions of the Bible that they found offensive and inimical to their cause; to add fuel to the fire, Garrison burned copies of the Constitution in public. Few actions provided the opponents of abolitionism with a more potent symbol of the dangerous nexus of religious ideas of freedom, unless they were those of a messianic slave rebel such as Nat Turner.

When faced with the most deeply difficult and morally contentious issue of the antebellum era, the evangelical synthesis fell apart; its center could not hold. The paradoxes and contradictions of being a slaveholding Christian Republic proved unsustainable. The irony was that in defending the trust in Christian republican ideas and commonsense readings of the sacred word, and later in fighting a war that may have included one of the most devout and Christianized sets of armies of any contest in modern history, it was American religious thought as it had been known and powerfully purveyed for the preceding century that was dealt a most grievous blow.

Noll's argument explains much, but to it might be added a consideration of the wider context of proslavery thought within the framework of nineteenth-century conservatism. The top ranks of southern theologians outlined a powerful proslavery argument based not on extrabiblical notions of racism but instead founded on a theological defense of European conservative ideas of social order. Good order pleased God; anarchy and theological infidelity did not.[35] Conservative theologians of both regions developed and presented a coherent and biblical proslavery argument that could not be refuted successfully with the commonsense biblical principles of the day.

To be sure, the proslavery argument relied on the evangelical synthesis to make its points. As one religious southern proslavery writer put it for *DeBow's Review* in 1850, "What we have written is founded solely upon the Bible, and can have no force, unless it is taken for truth. If that book is of divine origin, the holding of slaves is right; as that which God permitted, recognized and commanded, cannot be inconsistent with his will." Answering the argument that slavery in the Bible somehow differed from racial chattel slavery that enriched planters who sold goods raised by slaves in the international marketplace of commodities, the author insisted that in fact "the condition of the servant of the Roman empire, was much less free than that of the southern negro." Even as biblical masters had much more control, yet the Apostle Paul still insisted that servants were to submit to their masters—"not only to the good and gentle, but to the forward; and to masters to give to their servants what is just and equal." Both testaments of the Bible did not condemn the relation of slave and master but expressly allowed it and gave "commands and exhortations, which are based upon its legality and propriety. It can not, then, be wrong." Baptist minister Thornton Stringfellow of Virginia furthered this point, insisting that not only did the Bible not condemn slavery but that Paul's letters and the writings of Peter said "much to secure civil subordination to the State, and hearty and cheerful obedience to the masters, on the part of servants." It would seem from the biblical texts, then, that the true "danger to the cause of Christ" came from the side of *"insubordination among the servants*, and a *want of humility with inferiors*, rather than *haughtiness among superiors* in the church." If the cause of Christ suffered, in other words, it was the slaves' fault.[36]

The sermon in defense of slavery became a religious ritual of self-defense in the antebellum South. These exegeses outlined a conception of religion and freedom in America that drew deeply from the republican-evangelical synthesis while also upholding historically conservative views of hierarchy. It was a tense balance whose center ultimately would not hold. And yet for some time it drew the respect of national intellectual elites and also spoke to Americans of both sections who feared disorder both theological and social.

James Henley Thornwell's "The Christian Doctrine of Slavery" shows the genre at its intellectual peak. Thornwell was a southern gentleman theologian. Well-educated, urban, urbane, a college president, he represented the height of clerical achievement in the Old South. Born in 1812 as the son of a slave overseer in South Carolina, he took a degree from South Carolina College and studied theology briefly in New England. Throughout his life, he defended Presbyterian and Calvinist orthodoxy against the inroads of theological innovation. He defended his native land against abolitionist attacks, as well, and developed a reputation as the foremost intellectual defender of slavery and of southern ideas of freedom.

Thornwell delivered this particular sermon in honor of a new church structure for slave converts erected in Charleston in 1850. Its construction, he said, showed that southerners were faithful in "providing the Negro with the armor of salvation." "The Christian Doctrine of Slavery" specifically abjured racist theology. "I am not ashamed to call him [the Negro] my *brother*," Thornwell famously intoned to the audience. He reminded listeners that in Charleston, site of an abortive slave revolt to have been led by a black Methodist named Denmark Vesey in 1822, whites had been "warned by experience to watch, with jealous care, all combinations of blacks." He suggested that religious assemblies had been "so often prostituted to the unhallowed purposes of anarchy and crime, that good men began to apprehend that religion itself might be ultimately excluded" by white authorities fearful of black gatherings. But on this occasion, Charlestonians exemplified their commitment to "make known His Gospel, in its simplicity and purity, without any checks or hindrances," recognizing that "the doctrines of Jesus are doctrines according to godliness." Time would show, he assured his listeners, that the church would "prove a stronger fortress against insubordination and rebellion than weapons of brass or iron."[37]

Abolitionists such as William Ellery Channing in the North had made the argument that slavery denied man his humanity, turning him into an object, a "thing." Thus, slavery was wrong, for it denied the basic humanity of the slave. Thornwell, in response, insisted that the slave enjoyed "the same humanity in which we glory as the image of God." Slaves had a conscience, the fundamental constitutive element of human nature. Their conscience could not be owned, bartered, or exchanged. Just as slaves "owned" their own arms and legs, so they possessed their own minds. Thus, slavery could not in fact divest slaves of their humanity. What, then, was slavery? It was, Thornwell said, the obligation to "labour for another, determined by the Providence of God, independently of the provisions of a contract." Slave owners owned not slaves but the labor of their servants. Slavery remained a relationship between two sentient and moral beings, each endowed with the conscience with which God fitted all humanity. Slavery was a relationship of man to man, not man to things.[38]

What, then, were the social obligations imposed by this human relationship? Thornwell answered that men's duties depended on their particular social station in life. Thus, the Apostle Paul suggested to slaves that their obligations to their masters were the same as duties to God, "that a moral character attaches to their works, and that they are the subjects of praise or blame according to the principles upon which their obedience is rendered." And slaveholders had their own moral obligation "of rendering to their bondmen that which is just and equal." New Testament writings, Thornwell argued, recognized both the humanity and responsibilities of servants and masters. God's law was written on the conscience and the heart. It was man's obligation to discover and follow it. For slave owners, conscience dictated the just treatment of slaves. Likewise, for slaves, the conscientious following of duties should arise naturally from the moral sense. A fair and strict reading of the Bible demanded such an interpretation. "We are neither to question nor to doubt," Thornwell said, "but simply to interpret and believe." By following the law of God, slavery could be sanctified.[39]

Thornwell's generation developed the defense of slavery with a sophisticated blend of theological and social arguments. For them, slavery was not just a necessary evil. It could be a positive good in itself, provided that slaves received proper Christian treatment from their masters and paid due obedience in return. Slavery was not inherently good or evil; rather, any social order was godly or not godly, depending on how much men made it conform to God's image. If southern slave owners indeed abused their slaves, broke up families with impunity, and denied them the gospel message, then slavery in the United States should be abolished. But this was not the case, Thornwell argued, or at least it was not the norm. Instead, slave owners recognized and honored their God-given duties to their social inferiors. They cared for the servants, treated them as part of their family, and extended to them the same blessed message of Gospel freedom. Slavery was one of the curses that man's sin had brought into the world. But slavery could also be turned into a blessing when the institution inculcated a strong sense of the cheerful and obedient performance of social duties, a virtue necessary for civilization.

Thornwell and his colleagues, then, were essentially social conservatives. Their understanding of religion, freedom, and submission arose from that. They believed that human institutions had been passed down for good reason and could not be altered on a whim without inviting social disorder and chaos. Freedom depended on order; indeed, it arose from order. Disorder undermined that freedom. This is precisely what they saw in the North, and they blamed abolitionists and religious leaders alike for the emerging social disaster. By the 1830s and 1840s, more theologically liberal northerners had begun to break away from the heritage of conservative moral philosophy and to embrace broader readings of the Bible. Hence they argued that, even though certain passages in the Bible literally read did suggest that slaves should obey their masters, God's higher law, which humans could understand through a deeper and less literalist reading of the Bible, demanded a revolution in inequitable human relations. Many abolitionists accordingly fought not only against slavery but also for women's rights and suffrage. They also participated in the huge variety of reform movements and utopian dreams that arose in the antebellum North, ranging from reform of mental institutions to social experiments in communal living to spiritualism and other religious practices outside the Protestant mainstream. Repelled by this social and theological experimentation, southern conservatives returned to the Bible and commonsense realist assumptions to defend social order, evangelical theology, patriarchy, and slavery.

Thornwell's address came at a key moment in the years leading to the Civil War, when he could reasonably hope to persuade members of the Christian public to his view and when southern clerics could pronounce proslavery views with some confidence. Thornwell provided the divine imprimatur that many white southerners sought for their peculiar institution and later for their momentous decision to fight the bloodiest war in the nation's history to defend it. Thornwell died in 1862, three years before he could have witnessed God's verdict on the institution of slavery in the United States. The connections he drew between religious thought and social subordination exerted a long-lasting influence.

Beyond Thornwell, southern proslavery sermons preached from innumerable pulpits served the usual ritual purposes of exhortations to repentance, calls to hope, exultations in victory, lamentations in defeat, and identification of Confederates with God's will. Benjamin Morgan Palmer, the New Orleans Presbyterian and nationally known ministerial authority, outlined his conception of the South's specially appointed mission. Each nation, he argued, possesses its own "precisely defined character, fulfils its appointed mission, is developed through providential training, and is held to a strict providential reckoning." This was evident with the nations emanating from the sons of Noah. Hebrew history hinged on Noah's son Shem, progenitor of the Jewish people. Southerners, descendants of the people of Japheth, would be held to a similar standard: "Enlargement was promised to Japhet; and through all the past, the hardy and aggressive families of this stock have spread over the larger portion of the earth's surface, fulfilling their mission as the organ of human civilization." God gave the task of civilizing the world to the families of the stock of Japheth, while consigning the sons of Ham to the "doom of perpetual servitude." Since the biblical age, the progeny of Ham had failed to lift themselves above the "savage condition." God had placed his hand upon nations not just in appointing the "bounds of their habitations" but also in impressing upon each the "type of character that fits it for its mission."[40] In this case, even a gentleman theologian could not resist a full frontal assault on the cursed genealogy of blacks, and therefore the God-given right of whites, to impose order.

Religious Ideas of Freedom among the Slaves

The incessant emphasis on obedience in white sermons to the slaves drew much derision among slaves themselves, as evidenced by the frequency with which former slaves rebuked this hypocrisy. "When Nat Turner's insurrection broke out," a former Virginia slave recalled, "the colored people were forbidden to hold meetings among themselves.... Notwithstanding our difficulties, we used to steal away to some of the quarters to have our meetings."[41] Enslaved Christians might have attended white-sanctioned and supervised services and listened to white ministers advise them to obedience, patience, and humility. But they also created their own covert religious culture with its own distinctive theology and rituals. In services held in slave cabins, in the woods at night, and in "hush arbors," enslaved African Americans developed a religious culture that brought together elements of their African past and their American evangelical training. After the Civil War, the invisible church would become visible, as African-Americans formed thousands of their own churches and denominational institutions. Before the war, however, when such independent institutions were impossible, religious life emerged most clearly in the religious rituals of their own services, including ring shouts, spirituals, and chanted sermons.

African-American ideas of religious freedom arose in a context of white monitoring and control, the spread of Christianity, and the conversion of Christianity by African Americans into forms recognizable and meaningful to them. "Us went to de white folk's church," one ex-slave remembered, "an' set on back seats, but didn't jine in de worship. You see, de white folks don't get in de spirit, dey don't shout, pray, hum, and sing all through de services lak us do."[42]

Mostly denied the written Word, slave preachers mastered the arts of oral religious expression, sometimes publicly in separately organized black churches that remained under close white monitoring. In public their message was carefully contained. In private, however, when slaves spread the gospel among themselves, the preaching took flight. One black Texas minister, told by the master to preach obedience, subverted that message when he could: "I knew there was something better for them but I darsn't tell them so lest I done it on the sly. That I did lots." He told the slaves, "but not so Master could hear it, if they kept praying that the Lord would hear their prayers and set them free."[43] Antebellum slave preachers thus became agents of covert proselytization, precisely what Charles Colcock Jones's critics feared would happen.

While such preaching about the liberation of slaves was usually covert, in a few instances it was overt, and bloody. If Jesus was a trickster of the trinity, then his most potent and vengeful trickery came in the form of Nat Turner. Instigator of the short, violent, bloody rebellion in Southampton County, Virginia, in August 1831, Turner impressed whites as literate, quick, and intelligent. He scared them, too, for he espoused messianist visions of his God-given mission to purge the land with blood. From his younger years, as he recounted to a number of sources, he understood that God had given him a special spiritual purpose. As a young man, reflection on the verse from the Gospel of Matthew, "Seek ye the kingdom of Heaven and all things shall be added unto you," had persuaded him that the same "Spirit that spoke to the prophets in former days" now had come to him. He prayed continually and experienced the "same revelation, which fully confirmed me in the impression that I was ordained for some great purpose in the hands of the Almighty." He felt a communion with his fellow slaves. It was produced, he made clear, not "by the means of conjuring and such like tricks—for to them I always spoke of such things with contempt," but instead by the "communion of the Spirit whose revelations I often communicated to them, and they believed and said my wisdom came from God."[44]

While preparing himself for his God-given work, Turner received visions from the skies, revealing to him the intentions of the Holy Ghost. In 1828, he heard a loud noise in the sky, and "the Spirit instantly appeared" to him "and said the Serpent was loosened, and

Christ had laid down the yoke he had borne for the sins of men, and that I should take it on and fight against the Serpent." The time was approaching when the last would be made first. Asked if he still thought so given his imprisonment and impending execution, he asked simply, "was not Christ crucified?" The *Constitutional Whig*, a paper in Virginia, suggested that he was "perhaps misled by some hallucination of his imagined spirit of prophecy," while correspondents for the *Richmond Enquirer* described the person "at the bottom of this infernal brigandage" as a "fanatic preacher by the name of Nat Turner who had been taught to read and write, and permitted to go about preaching in the country." A general in search of him explained to the *Richmond Enquirer* that Turner had declared himself to his comrades as "commissioned by Jesus Christ" and inspired by divine direction and "that the late singular appearance of the Sun was the sign for him."[45]

Later in September, a report from the *Constitutional Whig* of Richmond, probably authored by Thomas R. Gray, Turner's lawyer and the amanuensis for what became Nat Turner's *Confessions*, pinned blame for the insurrection partly on the egalitarian religious fanaticism prevalent in the Commonwealth among both white and black. "Is it possible for men, debased and degraded as they are, ever to concert effective measures," he asked. Could slaves alone organize a general uprising? No, he answered, for in the British and Spanish colonies it took the "march of intellect among the free blacks" to foment revolution among the bondspeople. Virginia's slaves lacked such an organizing force—at least for now. But Gray apprehended danger to come precisely because evangelical doctrines and preachers full of "*ranting cant* about equality" confused spiritual and temporal freedom and thus threw Virginians into turmoil:

> But if any desire there was to increase this spirit among our slaves, I would advise our citizens, to permit coloured preachers to go on, as they have for several years past haranging vast crowds, when and where they pleased, the character of their sermons known only to their congregations—Nor do I think some of our white brethren, exempt from censure, when they fill their discourses with a *ranting*

cant about equality.—If our insurrection was known, beyond the neighborhood of its commencement—its cause must be attributed to the misguided zeal of good men, preaching up equality; and to ignorant blacks, who again retail the same doctrine, with such comments, as their heated imaginations may supply, to their respective circles of acquaintance.—For my own part, I think when a minister goes into a pulpit, flies into a passion, beats his fist, and in fine, plays the blockhead, that he gives a warrant to any negro who hears him, to do whatever he pleases provided his imagination, can make God sanction it.⁴⁶

The "ranting cant of equality"—the trickster tale of evangelicalism—also plagued the governor of Virginia, John Floyd, who conveyed similar sentiments about the dangers of democratic religious thought. In a letter to the governor of South Carolina, Floyd first blamed "Yankee peddlers and traders" for the "spirit of insubordination" in the state. They began sowing those seeds, he said, by "telling the blacks, God was no respecter of persons—the black man was as good as the white—that all men were born free and equal—that they cannot serve two masters—that the white people rebelled against England to obtain freedom, so have the blacks a right to do." Ministers from both sections, but principally from the North, persuaded respectable churchgoing people "that it was piety to teach negroes to read and write, to the end that they might read the *Scriptures*—many of them became tutoresses in Sunday schools and, pious distributors of tracts, from the New York Tract Society." Blacks then gathered and read or heard the "incendiary publications" of David Walker, William Lloyd Garrison, and others: "these too with songs and hymns of a similar character were circulated, read and commented upon." Meanwhile, the white populace rested in "apathetic security" until Turner's rampage. The governor was convinced that "every black preacher in the whole country east of the Blue Ridge was in the secret, that the plans as published by those Northern presses were adopted and acted upon by them—that their congregations, as they were called knew nothing of this intended rebellion, except for a few leading and intelligent men, who may have been head men in the Church—*the mass* were prepared by making them aspire to an equal station by such conversations as I have related as the first step." For Floyd, as for Gray, Turner's revolt foretold the results of how democratic religion and fanatical theology would revolutionize social and racial hierarchies in the United States.[47]

Turner was the rare exception. Perceptive whites understood that slaves could bide their time, dissemble before old Master, and otherwise do what had to be done in the short run while looking for signs of freedom in the longer run. Less perceptive whites took this to be contentment or believed that the slaveholders had truly made a world governed by Christian doctrine and planter paternalism. The truth was more complex than either view, actually, for slaves used the tools at their disposal—most especially, song—to work out philosophical questions about freedom.

More than anyplace else, the slaves articulated their theology of religion and freedom in the spirituals (as explored in greater detail in chapters 1 and 3). The spirituals, as poetry and literature set in musical form, took on many meanings, depending on the time and circumstance and individual. For generations of slaves, there was simply no viable hope that freedom would come in this life. But in times of turmoil and war, when the very future of slavery was in question, songs about freedom took on more obvious meanings. The remarkable rapidity with which slaves took up the story of the enslaved Israelites in Egypt as their own (despite the attempts of slave masters to prevent these passages in the Bible from being taught) shows that many had to be aware of the multiple meanings of what they sang. "Go Down Moses," with its exhortation to tell Pharaoh to release the captives in Egypt, may be the best example here. During the Civil War, whites jailed slaves in South Carolina for singing obviously subversive lines such as "We'll soon be free." Recording these lines, a white Union army officer who commanded a black regiment wrote that "though the chant was an old one, it was no doubt sung with redoubled emphasis during the new events." As one of his soldiers told him, "'Dey tink *de Lord* mean for say *de Yankees*,'" and that the final river to cross was not really the Jordan river of biblical times but the Potomac river into Washington.⁴⁸

The powerful proslavery theological impulse overmatched the abolitionist arguments, which were compelled to search outside the Bible. It did, however, meet its match in African American providentialism, in the black counternarrative that ran through the antebellum era, from David Walker's *Appeal* through the slave spirituals and into the events of the Civil War as interpreted through a millennialist prism.

Antislavery advocates found their most powerful public voice in Frederick Douglass. After escaping from his Maryland plantation in the 1830s, Douglass embarked on a remarkable career as an internationally known evangelist for human freedom. A brilliant writer and polemicist, Douglass was probably the single most effective proselytizer for the antislavery cause. In the 1840s and 1850s, while residing in Rochester and publishing the black abolitionist organ the *North Star*, he rhetorically devastated the slave system and the so-called revivalism that accompanied the spread of the iniquitous institution. As Douglass told one gathering, "Revivals in religion, and revivals in the slave trade, go hand in hand together. The church and the slave prison stand next to each other, the groans and cries of the heartbroken slave are often drowned in the pious devotions of his religious master . . . while the blood-stained gold goes to support the pulpit, the pulpit covers the infernal business with the garb of Christianity." In his first autobiography, Frederick Douglass famously condemned the religion of the slaveholding class. The same man who wielded the "blood clotted cowskin during the week fills the pulpit on Sunday," Douglass exclaimed, claiming all the while to be a "minister of the meek and lowly Jesus. The man who robs me of my earnings at the end of each week meets me as a class-leader on Sunday morning, to show me the way of life, and the path of salvation. He who sells my sister, for purposes of prostitution, stands forth as the pious advocate of purity." Douglass was a master at portraying slaveholders who blithely betrayed the principles of the meek and lowly Jesus. Douglass devastated the hypocritical pieties of white southern slaveholding religion, in part through his famous mocking imitations of white southern preachers, as recounted in this episode from a meeting he addressed:

> But what a mockery of His religion is preached at the South! I have been called upon to describe the style in which it is set forth. And I find our ministers there learn to do it at the northern colleges. I used to know they went away somewhere I did not know where, and came back ministers; and this is the way they would preach. They would take a text—say this:—"Do unto others as you would have others do unto you." And this is the way they would apply it. They would explain it to mean, "slaveholders, do unto *slaveholders* what you would have them do unto you:"—and then looking impudently up to the slaves' gallery, (for they have a place set apart for us, though it is said they have no prejudice, just as is done here in the northern churches;) looking high up to the poor colored drivers, and the rest, and spreading his hands gracefully abroad, he says, (mimicking,) "And you too, my friends, have souls of infinite value—souls that will live through endless happiness or misery in eternity. Oh, *labor diligently* to make your calling and election sure. Oh, receive into your souls these words of the holy apostle—'Servants, be obedient unto your masters.' (Shouts of laughter and applause.) Oh, consider the wonderful goodness of God! Look at your hard, horny hands, your strong muscular frames, and see how mercifully he has adapted you to the duties you are to fulfill! (continued laughter and applause) while to your masters, who have slender frames and long delicate fingers, he has given brilliant intellects, that they may do the *thinking*, while you do the *working*." (Shouts of applause.) It has been said here at the North, that the slaves have the gospel preached to them. But you will see what sort of gospel it is:—a gospel which, more than chains, or whips, or thumb-screws, gives perpetuity to this horrible system.[49]

Douglass continued with a condemnation of those who, "instead of preaching the Gospel against this tyranny, rebuke, and wrong," sought "by all and every means, to throw in the background whatever in the Bible could be construed into opposition to slavery, and to bring forward that which they could torture into its support."[50]

The white evangelical South of the nineteenth century faced a formidable competitor in the war for the American mind: the powerful sense that the Civil War represented a new era of human freedom to replace the bygone days of servitude. With this would come a true religion of Jesus to replace the Pharisaical one espoused by the southern slaveholders.

Conclusion: Southern Jesus and Southern Freedom

To return to our beginning: one of the most—maybe *the* most— fundamental paradoxes and tensions of American religious history is the fault line between religious freedom and democracy on the one hand and religiously sanctioned intolerance and repression on the other. Both come from American republican providentialism; that which is most honorable and that which is most execrable in the dominant story of American religion emerge from the same source. African Americans exploited this deeply contradictory impulse in American religion and in American life more generally. Thus, the explosively providentialist and universalist rhetoric of the Second Great Awakening, including Finneyite revivalism and the more intellectual formulations of the neo-Edwardseans, emerged alongside works forgotten or submerged or repressed, such as David Walker's *Appeal*, his cri de couer against the base hypocrisy of American Christianity; or of Henry Highland Garnet's 1843 plea for a nation of Nat Turners—a rejection of nonviolence so radical that Frederick Douglass denounced it in favor of a continued appeal to the biblical common sense of good Americans.

Democratic politics and the rapid rise of populist Christian sects created a new context for American ideas of religio-political freedom. The ebullient expressions of popular nationalism and the expansive and millennialist visions of religious groups such as the Methodists empowered a democratic culture and challenged the more deferential and hierarchical cast of American thought and life in prior decades. Thomas Jefferson's dream of a secular rationalist Republic had been replaced with something more akin to a Methodist millennium.

From the underside of that millennium, however, American ideas of freedom promised universalist visions but delivered a Republic that was, in practice, racially exclusivist and white supremacist. That paradox lay at the heart of native and African American religious thought and practice. Just as the Declaration of Independence became a touchstone for African American thought, both as a positive and a negative reference point, the universalist language of democratic Christianity provided a base for alternative visions of American ideas of freedom.

Religious freedom, democracy, and republicanism fostered religiously based repression. They also empowered counternarratives and grassroots struggles based on precisely the same evangelical premises. God must work in mysterious ways, for the line from religious freedom to theologically justified repression cycles back. In southern religious history, the repressed have returned to the dominant providentialist language to condemn biblically *and* extrabiblically based racist exercises in repressive power. Through American history, they have shined a harsh light on the dark places, particularly those places in the South, unsuccessfully hidden amid the city set upon the hill.

Religion, race, and southern ideas of freedom emerged from battles in slavery over the degree to which the message of Christianity was racialized versus the degree to which it was universal. African Americans from the early eighteenth century insisted on accessing the universalist language of Jesus; they made Jesus their own. Even when Jesus was conceived in apparently racialized terms—most often as a "small white man"—he was a trickster Jesus, a "subversive savior," who escaped the bounds of white supremacist religious thought.[51]

At the same time, white southern theologians too claimed Jesus as their own and constructed an impressive theological edifice that formulated ideas of spiritual freedom based on a social hierarchy maintaining civil and social order. Race, place, and station defined the white southern idea of religious freedom; the intersection of spiritual and temporal freedom, with Christianity as the leveler between the two, defined the black southern notion. Religion, race, and southern ideas of freedom, then, involved a classic philosophical clash between "negative" and "positive" liberty, to use philosopher Isaiah Berlin's terms. Did Christianity leave us free from sin but otherwise limited to pursue life within our given place in the social order; or did Christianity leave us free to pursue dreams and aspirations regardless of the social order into which we had been placed?

This philosophical quarrel extended to the level of religious practice. What constituted Christianity in practice? Certainly it included hymn singing, and it could even tolerate some emotional display. From the white southern perspective, it certainly did not include "paganisms," religious ritual imported from other continents or belief systems, including ring shouts, sung sermons, and "falling out."

In the free Republic, no federal establishment collected taxes for the support of a church, and the First Amendment protected the free exercise of religious belief. Of course, all of these were understood within a Christian, and often more specifically within a Protestant, context. Black believers were largely Protestant, yet they were often not defined as Christian, meaning their practices were outside the bounds of tolerability. Even more fascinating, black Christian leaders after the Civil War increasingly took it upon themselves to enforce norms of Christian order and respectability. Ultimately, their efforts met partial success at best, for the nexus of religion, race, and freedom could not be contained within the de facto culture of white Protestantism. The center of that moral establishment could not hold.

CHAPTER THREE

Suffering Saint

Jesus in the South

As perfectly portrayed by Robert Duvall, the character Sonny in the film *The Apostle* stands as one of the most memorable creations of the cinematic history of American religion. A Holiness minister of a biracial church in a southeastern Texas city, Duvall's Sonny exudes charisma, "Holy Ghost Power," and raw sexuality. His wife has left him for a "puny-assed youth minister"; aligned with his estranged wife, some members of the church have staged a successful coup against Sonny, ousting him from his pulpit. Torn about losing his children, Sonny visits his church one last time. In an apparent act of forgiveness and blessing, he hugs the new minister and some members while a raucous biracial band and choir scream out a Pentecostal praise anthem of Jesus, "He's All Right." Some time later at his son's baseball game, an enraged Sonny gulps some liquor from his flask and, in a momentary act of rage, fatally bludgeons the youth minister.

With the help of a friend he once converted from a life of alcoholism and crime, Sonny escapes from town, ditches his car in a creek, and sets out on foot across bayou country. Eventually he lands in a small Louisiana town. Quickly ingratiating himself with the townsfolk, Sonny puts his multiple talents to use: rebuilding the church structure, rejuvenating an old junker into a church bus, and chanting sermons over the local AM airwaves. Calling himself just "the Apostle," or "E.F.," and evading all questions about his background, Sonny seeks to redeem his life before the lawmen catch up to him, as inevitably they do. Before the police take him away, however, the Apostle E. F. leaves his parishioners with one memorable sermon, imploring the Lord to "give me peace."

Throughout the film, Duvall's character moves easily between white and black congregations and parishioners. At a Holiness/Pentecostal ministerial convention, Sonny and a black compatriot shout questions to the crowd: "Who's the King of Kings? Who's the everlasting one?" The biracial audience of ministers rhythmically replies, "Jesus." By the end, the film suggests, Sonny just might have saved himself. As the end credits roll, Sonny leads his fellow inmates working in the field with chants of "Jesus," their calls and responses marking time as they perform convict labor by the side of a road under the watchful gaze of guards.[1]

Sonny is at once passionately tender and threateningly violent. Seeming to walk straight from the pages of Wilbur J. Cash's *Mind of the South*, he is the Puritan and the hedonist, as quick to pull out the Bible as to bring up his fists or draw a gun.

As a young journalist, Wilbur J. Cash penned *The Mind of the South* in 1941, a brilliantly poetic, analytical cri de couer against the sentimentalized version of the old South, then being unforgettably disseminated in the film *Gone with the Wind*. Cash described the cinematic landmark as a "sort of new confession of the Southern faith." His work explored the cultural origins of the plain folk and the planter class. As they moved restlessly to populate the region in the antebellum era, they traced almost exactly the westward and southward movement of slavery. From its earliest days, Cash explained, southern evangelicalism tied together sin, subordination, and salvation with a "personal God, a God for the individualist, a God whose representatives were not silken priests but preachers risen from the people themselves."[2]

Like Wilbur J. Cash, Johnny Cash and a host of musicians, poets, and novelists of the South recognized the centrality of evangelical Protestantism in a region "haunted by God," one where believers hungered for a "personal Jesus." William Faulkner, hardly renowned for adherence to evangelical morality, acknowledged how he "assimilated" the South's religious tradition, taking "that in without even knowing it. It's just there. It has nothing to do with how much I might believe or disbelieve—it's just there."[3]

Jesus, too, was just there; in fact, he was everywhere. Writing in the same period as Faulkner, social critic Lillian Smith suggested that "God and Negroes and Jesus and sin and salvation" were "baled up together" in the minds of southerners. The fictitious apostle Sonny; the partly real, partly fictional persona of Johnny Cash; the tortured social observer Wilbur J. Cash; and the penetrating social critic Lillian Smith shared a tradition. They understood emotional evangelicalism as fundamental to a southern psyche torn between hedonism and guilt, as likely to take up the bottle or the knife as to break down in tears at a revival meeting. "What our Southerner required . . . was a faith as simple and emotional as himself," Wilbur J. Cash wrote in one of his exaggerated but trenchant summaries.[4]

Like Wilbur J. Cash, most modernist southern intellectuals derided the established regional evangelicalism that had long since made its peace with the reigning authorities. Jesus appeared as a complacent southerner, reduced to pronouncing a divine imprimatur on the region's peculiar institutions, from slavery through segregation. Radical ministers in the region cried out against such a powerless symbol. "Will the churches of the South," a progressive southern Congregational minister asked in 1945, "whose denominational roots are revolutionary and whose Holy Book is not a stick of candy but a stick of dynamite, . . . bring to the farm and factory worker a good wage, a decent house, a free assembly, a brotherhood enfolding all races?" In the rural South, where Depression set in well before the 1930s, angry clerics such as Owen Whitfield preached a revolutionary Jesus whose actions demanded a redress of the grievances of ordinary farmers being driven off the land during the New Deal era. "A sermon sends you home happy," he believed, while "the Gospel sends you home mad." Some striking coal miners in Kentucky in the 1930s saw the arrival of union leader John Lewis as the coming of Christ to their embattled mining towns. A coterie of students from southern backgrounds, notably including

Howard Kester and Myles Horton, learned of this radical Jesus from Reinhold Niebuhr, and they took that Jesus back to their work as southern subversives during the New Deal era and after, training labor and civil rights leaders at Highlander Folk School. Horton learned "from Jesus and the prophets" about the "importance of loving people, the importance of being a revolutionary, standing up and saying that this system is unjust. Jesus to me was a person who had the vision to project a society in which people would be equally respected, in which property would be shared . . . he was a person who said you have to love your enemies, you have to love the people who despise you."[5]

How did a region known originally for its indifference, for an unruly populace given more to partying than to praying, metamorphose into a Bible Belt famous for a fiery, visceral attachment to Jesus? One answer is that Jesus physically, viscerally, and symbolically resided in the central experiences of southern history. As the South became the Bible Belt, Jesus became a southerner. African Americans planted him squarely in the southern evangelical imagination. Once there, Jesus captured the hearts and minds of white southerners as well. Jesus as symbol defined the southern paradox of suffering and salvation. His mythical arc spoke powerfully, if differently, to whites and blacks. In the rise of the Confederacy and the Lost Cause and through the sanctification of segregation, white southerners imagined Jesus as their patron saint. In the radical religion of grassroots clerics such as Owen Whitfield and freelance social organizers such as Myles Horton, Jesus became a proto-revolutionary. In black southern church life, Jesus was a fellow sufferer who promised a social redemption.

As the most pious and Christianized, and as the most racially violent and inequitable, region of the country, southerners have turned to the pervasive Christ imagery all around them in private moments of reflection as well as during the most dramatic events of American history. Christ's truth marched on with the Confederate soldiers; their sacrifices were understood as expiation for regional sins. A lily-white Jesus pervaded the Lost Cause, and the film version of Thomas Dixon's *The Clansman* devastatingly employed an ethereal

Jesus to preside over the triumph of the Klan; He appeared as a "gentle Prince in the Hall of Brotherly Love in the City of Peace," superimposed over an all-white gathering celebrating the reconciling of the cleansed white nation. Jesus approved the very "peace among the whites" that Frederick Douglass feared would follow the salutary effects of the war among the whites.

Meanwhile, the black southern Christ, an apolitical suffering servant, inspired the greatest social uprising in twentieth-century American history: the civil rights movement. The Jesus of the black South represented the oppressed, the scourged, the downtrodden, and the lynched. As W. E. B. Du Bois put it in 1913, "Jesus Christ was a laborer and black men are laborers. He was poor and we are poor; He was despised of his fellow men and we are despised; He was persecuted and crucified and we are mobbed and lynched." Du Bois mined the connection between Jesus and black Americans: the suffering savior and suffering southerners. So did legions of black preachers, musicians, and artists.[6] The Jesus of African Americans may have appeared white in imagery and symbolism, but he became a black southerner in the act of suffering: an oppressed slave, a victim of a crucifixion-lynching, a poor migrant, a fellow-sufferer on the front lines of civil rights battles. Long before the rise of black theology in the civil rights era, slaves and freed African Americans imagined, painted, sermonized about, and musically portrayed a liberatory Jesus. For them, Jesus's white imagery belied his black sympathies.

The Southern Jesus sanctified suffering and assured triumph. He appeared in white and black guises; he transformed the region and individual souls; he led armies and rode milk-white horses; he materialized in the form of Civil War generals and civil rights leaders. In short, he entered both the white and black imaginary as a figure of immediate, tangible, enormous power. He soothed souls battered by slavery and segregation, and he provided inspiration for the most stunning social revolution of twentieth-century American history. Jesus as Southerner was a transformative figure, and as the South developed into the Bible Belt, that figure became associated with the region in the popular mind. From "Amazing Grace" to *Saving*

Grace, from *Christ in the Camp* to *Color Purple*, and from spirituals to country, blues, and soul, a racially divided but viscerally present Southern Jesus became the American Jesus.

Birth of the Southern Jesus

Christ imagery emerged slowly in American history. Jesus symbols did not spring from Puritans, whose theology effectively disallowed images of him. Visions of the Savior ebbed during the relative lull in religiosity around the time of the American Revolution. Once born in full form during the second Great Awakening, though, he spread quickly in the southern imagination. Southerners, white and black, envisioned Jesus powerfully in conversion experiences, dreams, and song. White and black imaginations of Jesus influenced each other, creating the regional evangelical style that eventually pervaded the southern countryside. Jesus's rise in the context of the slave South gave images of Christ a special resonance: Christ as suffering servant had an obvious analogue in slaves.

Southern white ministers in the antebellum era insisted that "Of one blood did he make all nations upon earth," as the Right Reverend William Meade intoned in his 1853 pastoral letter to Episcopalians in Virginia, and that "He sent his Son to taste death for every man." Jesus came, Meade believed, most especially for the poor: "our glorious Emmanuel chose the form of a servant, became the servant of servants, illustrating [Christianity's] blessed doctrines by his own meek, patient, suffering life." Reassuring whites of the safety of the mission to the slaves, Meade noted how Jesus had "adapted all his precepts and promises and doctrines to the poor, and those who were in bondage" and asked, "Where will you find a word that proceeded from his lips, which could excite pride, discontent, or rebellion? On the contrary, does not the whole spirit of the Gospel lead us to feel that the poorest and most oppressed condition upon earth is too good for such sinful beings as we all are." The words and image of Jesus, his example on earth, would speak to servants, for they were "admirably calculated to soothe a wounded spirit," and "reconcile" slaves to the "hardships of their lot."[7]

Southern missionaries sought examples in their own churches of how a true understanding of Jesus would reprove and instruct ordinary folk, especially slaves, whose religious visions sometimes strayed beyond proper theological order. One Catholic missionary in New Orleans boasted of his congregation of free people of color as well as enslaved persons, and a staff of church folk who catechized the black initiates. His black converts wore "a red ribbon and a cross" and promised "to fight daily like valiant soldiers of Jesus." He presided over Sunday gatherings, "regulate[d] their practice," and pronounced them faithful as seminarians. By such means, southern Catholic fathers hoped, God had snatched "thousands of children of the race of Canaan" from the "barbarity of their ferocious customs." One Catholic father hoped that "though their skins remain brown . . . their souls will soon be white."[8]

On occasion, the mission to the slaves seemed to work in conflating the slaveholders' reign with God's power. "I really believed my old master was almighty God," Henry "Box" Brown recalled, "and that his son, my young master, was Jesus Christ." When older, Brown realized the metaphorical truth of his apprehensions. Slaveholders, he grasped, really were like gods on the plantation. But by that time, he had long since literally boxed himself up and delivered himself to freedom in Philadelphia, an escape he detailed in his classic memoir *Narrative of Henry Box Brown, Who Escaped from Slavery Enclosed in a Box 3 Feet Long and 2 Wide.*[9]

To slaves, Jesus was more than conqueror for he intervened actively in the everyday lives of the lowliest servants of the South. More than a spirit, he was seeable, touchable, tangible. He walked on earth like a man, a suffering servant who channeled God's power. "When Christ walked on de water, de Apostles was skeered he was a spirit," one ex-slave reflected in his defense of the reality of spirits on earth, "but Jesus told dem dat he warn't no spirit dat he was as 'live as day was." Jesus listened to the agonies of sinners passing through the iron gates of spiritual death. Jesus's personal power overwhelmed any other on earth. That is why, Cordelia Jackson of South Carolina explained, white folks told "stories 'bout 'ligion. Dey tells stories 'bout it [because] dey's 'fraid of it. I stays independent of what white folks tells me when I shouts. . . . Never does it make no difference how I's tossed about. Jesus. He comes and save me everytime."[10]

Jesus's presence in bondspeople's excruciating encounters with the slave power runs through many narratives. Jesus appears in the midst of whippings and beatings, restraining unjust punishers and soothing wounded bodies. James Watkins was one of many who recounted his conversion experience at a camp meeting, where the minister spoke to a racially segregated crowd of "one Jesus who had told a blind man to go to the pool and wash, and he received his sight. Oh! I thought could I but find this Jesus! How I long to know him!" Watkins thought that "if I could but find out this great man I should be free from slavery as well as from sin." When he returned to the quarters, his master accosted him: "'You infernal black ghost, you have got no soul. I'll teach you to go to the Camp Meeting.'" Intending to give Watkins his whipping, the master succumbed to Watkins's prayers and pleadings, "till he trembled from head to foot like an aspen leaf." Watkins attributed his rescue to the intervention of Jesus. Martha Griffith Browne's vision of Jesus did not protect her from a beating but kept her soul together during her torment: "I saw the darkness and gloom that overshadowed the earth, when, deserted by His disciples, our blessed Lord prayed alone." She "heard the sighs and groans that burst from his tortured breast," saw the bloody sweat of his body and the grimaces of his inhuman captors, witnessed his face uplifted to the mournful Heavens, watched him bound and led away to death, and heard the nails pounded through his hand and the thorny crown pressed upon his brow. With the prophecy fulfilled, she then "beheld Him triumphing over the powers of darkness and death, when, robed in the white garments of the grave, He broke through the rocky sepulcher, and stood before the affrighted guards." The Reverend Noah Davis left a similar account in his 1859 memoir. At a revival meeting, he felt a weight even while he was joyful at heart. Then, "while trying to pray, I thought the Saviour appeared to me. I thought I saw God smiling upon me, through Christ, His Son. My soul was filled with love to God and Jesus Christ. It appeared to me, I saw fullness in

Jesus Christ, to save every sinner who would come to Him. And I felt, that if I was only converted, I would tell all sinners how precious the Saviour was."[11]

Some slaves, including Peter Randolph, did not so much see Jesus as feel him during a conversion. Seeking to acquire literacy, Randolph most wanted to read the Bible so he could live with Christ in heaven. He would "go into the woods and lie upon my back, and pray that he would come and take me to himself—really expecting to see Him with my bodily eyes." Later he felt that God would have mercy on him, and then "instead of looking with my real eyes to see my Savior, I felt him in me, and I was happy. The eyes of my mind were open, and I saw things as I never did before. With my mind's eye, I could see my Redeemer hanging upon the cross for me." But most of the slaves around him saw the Savior more physically than mentally:

> The slaves talk much of the sufferings of Christ; and oftentimes, when they are called to suffer at the hands of their cruel overseers, they think of what he endured, and derive patience and consolation from his example. Their ideas of him, however, are not very clear. They think that He is standing somewhere, looking at them with pitying eyes, and HE knows all about what is going on. They conceive of God as a very large man, with feet and hands, and eyes and ears, whose house is somewhere in the skies, and that He has books, and is always writing down what takes place on the earth. They expect to see Him as a man; and that HE will talk to them, if they will look for Him. They think Jesus to be inferior to God in size; and that the reason why He is so small is, that He once dwelt in the flesh, and was so badly treated as to hinder his growing large![12]

Again, the fact that Jesus was diminutive, as humans are small before God, spoke to a kind of identification with Christ. Believers in the house of bondage saw "Him as a man" during their sufferings in captivity. Slaves sang "O brother, where was you When the Lord come passing by? Jesus been here, O he's been here; He's been here / Soon in the morning; Jesus been here / And blest my soul and gone."[13]

Slaves identified his power being exercised through human means, including the Union army. "Master laugh one day," a black soldier from the Sea Islands recalled during the Civil War. "Ask me if I think Christ want black nigger in heaven. One thing, sure. We'uns going to be where the crucify Lord am. And if that place be Hell, He going to make it heaven for we." When news of freedom came to one slave, she could barely contain herself in front of the master: "I jump up and scream, 'Glory, glory hallelujah to Jesus! I'se free! I'se free!'" She felt "so full o' praise to Masser Jesus." The language of "Masser Jesus" spoke to her acceptance of the southern language of hierarchy, but its inversion as well.[14] Charlotte Forten, a black northern missionary volunteer in the Sea Islands during the war, heard the "rich tones" of black boatmen in 1864, singing in "sweet, strange, and solemn" voices: "Jesus makes de blind to see / Jesus make de cripple walk; Jesus make de deaf to hear. Walk in, Kind Jesus." They continued singing more Jesus songs: "Go down in de Lonesome Valley . . . to meet my Jesus dere!" . . . "Feed on milk and honey, my Lord, . . . Meet my Jesus dere!" And another, featuring warm greetings in Gullah dialect with a physically present King Jesus: "In de mornin' when I rise, Tell my jesus Huddy oh! / I wash my hands in de mornin' glory, Tell my Jesus Huddy oh!"[15] Northern Quaker Lucy Chase, though initially contemptuous of the emotionalism of the freedpeople, quickly learned their devotion in song to the Savior. As she quoted them to an abolitionist newspaper in 1863, "We often hear the negroes singing this—'Jesus been here, been here, been here—Dun bless my soul and gone.'"[16]

As commander of the First South Carolina Volunteers, a black regiment of the Union army, white abolitionist and literary figure Thomas Wentworth Higginson recorded some of the classic expressions of black testimony. For Higginson, slave theology exhibited "Nothing but patience for this life,—nothing but triumph in the next." Yet Higginson's own descriptions of his men's expressions contradicted this interpretation, for the men anticipated imminent triumph in this life through the graces of King Jesus and Father Abraham. His troops understood perfectly well that freedom was coming, and they saw Jesus at the head of the army ushering in the new era. "Ride in, kind Saviour!" he recorded his men singing around their campfires.

> No man can hinder me.
> O, Jesus is a mighty man!
> No man, &c.
> We're marching through Virginny fields.
> No man, &C.
> O, Satan is a busy man,
> No man, &c.
> And he has his sword and shield,
> No man, &c.
> O, old secesh done come and gone!
> No man can hinder me.

Higginson heard the classic exhortation to prepare one's soul for the Savior:

> Jesus call you. Go in de wilderness
> Go in de wilderness, go in de wilderness,
> Jesus call you. Go in de wilderness
> To wait upon de Lord.

The sufferings of slavery and the imminent coming of freedom could be found in another of the tunes:

> My brudder, how long (Thrice).
> 'Fore we done sufferin' here?
> We'll soon be free (Thrice.)
> When Jesus sets me free.
> We'll fight for liberty (Thrice).
> When de Lord will call us home.[17]

But with the coming of the war, Jesus's face could be seen. The slave could purge the guilty land by calling America back to a truer vision of Christ. In this way, the slaves' own sacrifice over generations of time, blood, and labor would serve the redemptive mission of purifying an America stained with the sin of crucifying its most Christ-like figures.[18]

The Death and Rebirth of the White Southern Jesus

By 1865, Ella Gertrude Clanton Thomas had been brought to her knees, in prayer and in defeat. As the pious slaveholding woman from Georgia was just beginning to realize, abolition had shown her "how intimately my faith in revelations and my faith in the institution of slavery had been woven together—true I had seen the evil of the latter but if the *Bible* was right then slavery *must be*—Slavery was done away with and my faith in God's Holy Book was terribly shaken. For a time I doubted God. The truth of revelations, all—everything."[19]

White southerners such as Thomas pondered this persistent dilemma: the Jesus of the Bible was a suffering servant, but the suffering servants of the South were Negro slaves. By this inexorable theological logic—the same one the abolitionists exploited, the same one enslaved Christians themselves identified with—Jesus was a black slave, and those abusive slaveholders who claimed to be followers of the meek and lowly Jesus were blasphemers. As the Civil War approached, and then as the fighting intensified into a death struggle, Jesus could be a warrior, leading the troops to battle even while comforting the afflicted (including wounded soldiers), and ensuring the righteousness of the conflict. Even so, Jesus as warrior could be a general for freedom as much as a preserver of the Southern Cause. His contradictory roles as suffering servant and crusading warrior accentuated the theological tension about Jesus in the South. The region really did have suffering servants, closely analogous to Jesus in that role, and they were not white. Christian abolitionists never tired of pointing this out.

The image of the suffering Jesus, of course, was readily adaptable, and so what may have appeared as a theological conundrum *for* the white South found a solution in the transformation of Jesus into a savior *of* the white South. The triumphant Jesus of the black southern imagination paralleled a Jesus of salvific consolation in the white southern imagination. Thus, Jesus was the patron saint of the Redemptionist Cause, and the Lost Cause. Like the South itself, He had laid down his life as an act of spiritual sacrifice, as had the

Confederate soldiers under the Christ-like leader Robert E. Lee; and as Jesus was resurrected, so might be a South viewed as a spiritual preserver of the nation. At the beginning of the war, Confederate Mildred Lynch wrote in her diary of attending a church service where the preacher made the congregants feel "the rest through Jesus, that remains for the people of God, and we were *comforted.* Oh! May the brave soldiers return to us, not only victorious, but may each one enlist under the banner of the Cross, and at last be enabled to say I have fought the good fight." Sarah Manly, wife of a founder of the Southern Baptist Convention, wrote to her three sons serving in the Confederate army: "I am humbly thankful that I have reason to believe that you have each enlisted under the banner of the cross of Jesus Christ. God knows that my greatest desire is (and has ever been) that you should be, sincere and consistent Christians." Future generations of white southerners would proclaim that their men had enlisted "under the banner of the Cross," and that their leaders, especially Robert E. Lee, had carried the Cross and thus in effect transfigured themselves into Christ figures.[20]

The northern Christ was a triumphant crusader, leading humanity closer to a universal freedom. The white southern Christ, by contrast, grew into a symbol of suffering for a higher form of purity. White southern ministers after the war frequently analogized the suffering South to the dying Christ. Just as Jesus was pierced by a crown of thorns before he was fitted with a crown of glory, so southerners would endure their suffering in a Christ-like way and emerge victorious. Nashville Presbyterian James I. Vance, for example, intoned that "his enemies could nail Christ to the cross, but they could not quench the ideals he embodied. His seemed to be a lost cause as the darknesss fell on the great tragedy at Calvary, but out of what seemed Golgotha's irretrievable defeat has come the cause whose mission it is to save that which is lost." Southerners did not yet understand what purpose God had for the war, another minister surmised, but trusted that "God is with us in this conflict; we think he is on our side in the struggle." Even evidences of reverses for the Confederate military fortunes simply signaled that "Our cause is sacred. It should ever be so in the eyes of all true men in the South. How can we doubt it, when we know it has been consecrated by a holy baptism of fire and blood." The southern cause was the cause of God, "of Christ, of humanity. It is a conflict of truth with error—of the Bible with Northern infidelity—of a pure Christianity with Northern fanaticism—of liberty with despotism—of right with might."[21]

Christian symbology pervaded Confederate camp revivals late in the war and thereafter underlay the theology of the "religion of the Lost Cause." From the hundreds of Confederate monuments setting in biblical relief the major southern war heroes, to the addresses at yearly Sons of Confederate Veterans and United Daughters of the Confederacy meetings, to the inscriptions on the monuments themselves, Jesus sanctified a unified white southern people who had fought for Him. In the process, Jesus was reclaimed (in part), for now his suffering was akin to that of the white South rather than to the servants of the slave South. "No nation rose so white and fair: None fell so pure of crime," reads the Confederate monument in Augusta, Georgia, erected as part of a building spree inspired by the efforts of the United Daughters of the Confederacy in the later nineteenth century. Key to this mythology was the exalting of southern war heroes as Christian evangelical gentleman. Evangelists of the New South era immortalized the Christian heroism of the Confederate leaders and soldiers and dovetailed them into revivals of the era.[22]

John William Jones's *Christ in the Camp*, first published in 1887, identified the Southern cause with Christ. More than anyone else, Jones connected revivalism in the southern army with a Jesus who struggled alongside the noble soldiers. In a sermon before veterans in 1900, Jones asked, "when the roll is called up yonder," would those present be prepared to "'cross over the river and rest under the shade of the trees' with Davis and Lee and Jackson and other Christian comrades who wait and watch for your coming?" While *Christ in the Camp* claimed that the revivals exalted Jesus and avoided "controversial" issues of the sectional conflict, the text demonstrated how much the cause of Christ became connected with the sanctification of the Confederacy. If northern memory of the conflict was secularized, especially by a postwar generation of philosophical pragmatists who had come to distrust religious devotion to transcendent causes, southern memorialists sacralized the war and the cause of the Confederacy.[23]

The ferocity of the war itself naturally turned men's thoughts to the divine. "Without a doubt," one southern soldier acknowledged, "in hundreds of instances, the shock of battle has been sanctified to the saving of souls." After revivals swept their camp, soldiers stationed for battle in Orange County, Virginia, steeled themselves for war with praises of Jesus. Wrote one correspondent, "Now, instead of the songs of revelry and mirth to which we used to listen, at night the forest is made to resound with songs which arise like sweet incense from new-born souls, to the Captain of their salvation—the stately stoppings of Jesus are heard in our camps—the Holy Spirit is wooing hearts in our army—soldiers are enlisting under the unfurled banner of King Immanuel." A chaplain for another regiment reported on the "blessed" reports from "men soon to march with martial tread to deal and receive fatal shot on the bloody field! How cheering is the thought that our liberties are defended by such soldiers!" Soldiers took comfort in feeling that they rested "safe in the arms of the Lord Jesus." They saw "Glorious brightness" that came "straight from my Saviour's countenance." Dying soldiers' stories fill *Christ in the Camp* and suggest how central images of Jesus had become to the dead and dying of the war. One correspondent for the Virginia *Religious Herald*, a Baptist newspaper, left an account of standing "by the bedside of one of the heroes who are daily offering themselves as sacrifices upon the altar of their country." As he "gazed upon the thin, emaciated form" of the soldier on the cot, he thought "'Jesus, the King of kings, dwells here, and I had rather be this poor soldier than to be the tenant of a palace.'" Death soon came to the soldier, "for when I heard from him again he had fallen asleep in Jesus . . . Oh, blessed Jesus! Oh, thou divine Redeemer! when we see our friends . . . free from fear because Thou art with them, we would raise our hearts and our voices in adoration, and praise, and thankfulness to Thee."[24]

Robert E. Lee's Christ-like qualities and dedication resounded through Lost Cause literature. As a Christ figure, morally spotless but betrayed by the sins of lesser men (General James Longstreet usually standing in for Judas in this story), he showed how a character could be honed to perfection by pain and how the South "had transformed the shame of its worldly failure into a glorious, metaphysical triumph." Lee was emblematic of the notion that "God's greatest gift to a race and a time is some one man in whom that race shall see the embodiment of its highest ideals." He lived not for himself but for his fellow men, for "the sign of the Cross was upon his life." At the dedication ceremony for the newly constructed Lee chapel at Washington (now Washington and Lee) College, Senator John W. Daniel of Virginia portrayed the fallen Confederate hero as "the Priest of his people," who drank "every drop of Sorrow's cup." The chapel, where Lee's remains rested, became a "holy place."[25]

The common soldier could stand in for Christ as well. While a figure like Lee was cast in marble, a model beyond compare but worthy of emulation, ordinary Confederate soldiers provided exemplars worthy of respect precisely because of their ordinariness. When caught by Union soldiers and executed in 1864, martyred Tennessean Sam Davis entered southern lore as a Confederate Christ:

> On Calvary the Son of God died with cruel nails driven through his quivering flesh, the crown of thorns pressing down on his agonized brow, and since then the cross has been the Christian's sign in every land; and which of us has the right to say that He who created the earth and the sky and every living thing on sea and land, whose mysteries baffle, but whose providence is over all, could give the Son of Mary to teach men how to live could not also give this son of Tennessee to teach men how to die.

Veterans' organizations propounded the Southern view of history—that Confederates fought not for slavery but for "liberty"; that Northern aggressors had threatened that liberty; that ordinary soldiers struggled heroically against insurmountable odds for their homeland; and that the cause of the Confederacy, though lost in 1865, would rise again, just as did Jesus. "When our Divine Master perished on the cross, did the doctrines for which he died die with him," asked former South Carolina general and Redemptionist politician Wade Hampton in 1892. The principles of the Confederacy were not lost, just as the cause of Christ had not been lost at Golgotha, said a former private in Lee's army: "Truth, subjected to mock trial and condemnation, scourged and spitted on, betrayed by secret foes, staggering under its Cross, and sealed to-day in its sepulchers, bursts tomorrow the gates of death, rises with the crown, triumphant reigns throughout the world."[26]

Thus, the southern war heroes came draped in Christ-like language, especially Robert E. Lee. And thus John William Jones in his classic of memorialized exaggeration, *Christ in the Camp*, could exalt the Confederate battalions as the most religious army since Cromwell's. "Jesus *was* in our camps with wonderful power," he knew. And thus, in a later period, white southerners could deliver invocations at nearly every public event, including United Confederate Veterans' gatherings as well as spectacle lynchings. Whites sought God's blessings on the expiation of communal sins through the sacrifice of black victims. Black bodies, burned in ceremonies both solemn as well as carnivalesque and sometimes later carved up by souvenir hunters, stood as an unforgettable testament to a southern obsession with purity. When those murders took place in churchyards, as was the case with the lynching of Harris Tunstal behind a white Methodist church in Oxford, Mississippi, in July 1885, Jesus was implicitly there, too. In this case, white congregants "from all walks of life" left their normal church preparations to watch Tunstal say his last prayers. The Mob "seemed to appreciate the fact that it was horrible work for the Sabbath day," according to one account, "and that they were sending a spirit illy prepared before his God, and realized that human life is sacred and a human soul divine, yet they knew that they had duties to perform and paramount to all others was the thought that *they must protect their women*." Jesus thus commanded it.[27]

And thus, too, southern novelist and social gospel minister Thomas Dixon could fill his works with calls for "righteous wrath," for "the love which filled the soul of Christ was a consuming fire, and before it evil must be burned up." Dixon had found success both as a social gospel orator and on the New York stage before embarking on his career as a novelist and mythmaker. He believed that "Jesus Christ was of the common people," but he also worried about the "dark, vulgar mass" of humanity who needed uplift from visionaries such as Dixon himself. In his novels, the "Invisible Empire" of the Klan became, in effect, the Church Militant, an analogy furthered by his sermon "The Larger Church," which suggested that "the church of Christ is an invisible empire."[28]

Thus, too, the white robes of the Invisible Empire in *Birth of a Nation*, the epochal 1915 film adapted from the stories in Dixon's novels, became a centrally produced and regulated uniform for the Second Ku Klux Klan, a real-life realization of an Invisible Empire that was now visible in public parades and spectacles. William J. Simmons, a minister largely responsible for re-creating the Second Ku Klux Klan at Stone Mountain, Georgia, in 1915, understood that Christ could serve as a central symbol for his order. The white Jesus already had ascended to prominence in larger cultural imagery, from the works of self-proclaimed defenders of the "Nordic race" such as Madison Grant's *The Passing of the Great Race* (1916) to the white masculine Christ of Bruce Barton's *The Man Nobody Knows* in 1924. The robes worn by members, one Alabama Klansmen assured listeners, were not emblems of secrecy or skullduggery but, rather, symbolized the purity of Jesus. The Klan would only unrobe when "rapists, thugs, gamblers, crooked politicians, and murderers no long encumber the earth."[29]

Klan publications in the 1920s adopted "the living Christ" as the "Klansman's criterion of character," as went the opening prayer of the officially prescribed Klan ritual of the 1920s. Klansmen were to emulate the Savior's example, for Jesus himself "was a Klansman," one Texan proclaimed. Christ was "a member of the oldest Klan in existence—the Jewish theocracy," one who "sought, first of all, to deliver the people of his own race, blood, and religion." Eventually Jesus created his own clan, that of Christianity itself, a religion based on moral character instead of other ties. Jesus's act upon the cross perfectly symbolized the Klan's turn to Jesus as the emblem of suffering, pain, service, and sacrifice, the very "criterion of character" spoken of in the Klan's own literature. "Since Jesus's wounded body bore the sins of the world," a Klan historian explained, "a member should follow Jesus's example. . . . It was not necessary to sacrifice one's life, but to sacrifice one's selfhood for the greater body of Klan membership."[30]

By the Great War and the early 1920s, Jesus was emblematic of a white South laid low by the depredations of Yankee troops and carpetbagging politicians during Reconstruction. He was at the center of Lost Cause theology and symbolically presided over rituals of purity that reassured white Southerners of their Redemption, both personal and political. The white Christ crucified during the war had been resurrected. As in D. W. Griffith's film, this white, southern Christ blessed the rebirth of the nation.

The Black Southern Jesus Confronts the White Christ

Disillusioned by their abandonment and by the surge in racist violence in the late nineteenth century, black ministers, activists, and politicians combed religious texts for explanation. The racialization of Christ into a symbol of white southern purity demanded radical countertheologies. Jesus had to return again, this time not in the guise of the Union Army but in the voices of black men. Henry McNeal Turner, a Union army chaplain and organizer for the African Methodist Episcopal Church in the South after the war, enunciated the idea best in his paper *Voice of Missions*, a sheet promoting African American missionary work in and emigration to Africa. "We have as much right Biblically and otherwise to believe that God is a Negro as you buckra, or white, people have to believe that God is a fine looking, symmetrical and ornamented white man," wrote Turner, whose tumultuous time as a Reconstruction state legislator in Georgia left him embittered about the prospects of equality for black Americans. "For the bulk of you, and all the fool Negroes of the country, believe that God is a white-skinned, blue-eyed, straight-haired, projecting-nosed, compressed-lipped and finely robed white gentleman, sitting upon a throne somewhere in the heavens," he cried. As did the Marcus Garveyites of the next generation, and a number of relatively unknown black ministers of his own generation, Turner understood that the racialization of the divine devastated freedpeople already imprinted with the stigma of slavery. Turner reshaped God in the image of blacks. "Every race of people since time began who have attempted to describe their God by words, or by paintings, or by carvings, or by any other form or figure, have conveyed the idea that the God who made them and shaped their destinies was symbolized in themselves, and why should not the Negro believe that he resembles God as much so as other people? We do not believe that there is any hope for a race of people who do not believe that they look like God."[31]

In an anthology of essays devoted to finding the meaning of Africa in an age of colonialism, Turner complained, "Everything that is satanic, corrupt, base and infamous is denominated *black*, and all that constitutes virtue, purity, innocence, religion, and that which is divine and heavenly, is represented as *white*." Turner argued biblically that "God is a Negro" while also insisting that "we are no stickler as to God's color." Most importantly for him, he protested against "God being a white man or against God being white *at all*."[32]

Black religious folk artists, entrepreneurs, literary figures, and essayists picked up Turner's themes in the early twentieth century. They wove black Christs into textiles, pictured him through paintings, wrote about him in literary works and theological treatises, and theologized about him in new churches and religious institutions. Black authors resurrected the hidden black story of the Bible and traced Jesus's African lineage. James Morris Webb, for example, explained how Jesus descended from Africans, and therefore "the blood of the Negro coursed through the veins of Jesus and Solomon." A native of Tennessee, Webb sold his book *The Black Man, the Father of Civilization* through black newspapers such as the *Chicago Defender*. In it, he traced the black genealogy of various Biblical characters. Besides the book, for an additional fee purchasers could get a "picture of Jesus as a Colored man with wooly hair and a book proving the same." In a sermon he recorded advertising his wares, Webb detailed how "the Bible shows that God did use Negro men and women in making biblical history." Like many nineteenth-century commentators, he rescued Ham from being the subject of a curse and reclaimed him as being the biblical father of the black men.[33] In similar fashion, W. L. Hunter's *Jesus Christ Had Negro Blood in His Veins: The Wonder of the 20th Century*, first published in 1901 and going through nine editions by 1913, discovered four black women in Christ's genealogy. Both Webb and Hunter followed the "begats" to discover Jesus's African lineage, usually through the mother's side, which could be traced to the Canaanites. They argued that Noah's son Ham and many biblical figures had African origins; thus, Jesus's descent could be traced to Africa. Hunter concluded that the "incarnate Savior was nearer a black than a white man, and if He was living in the United States of America today He would be called a negro." Hunter asked "Will the white man worship a black Savior? Yet, that is what they do every day in the week, and must forever do or have no Savior at all."[34]

From David Walker to Henry Turner and W. L. Hunter, black theologians excoriated the white God, represented on earth by a lily-white Jesus. This thought found its twentieth-century expression in works such as *Jesus Christ Had Negro Blood in His Veins*, by the "blackening" of Jesus through the rise of the gospel blues, and in fine and vernacular artists who envisioned black Christs before there was anything called black theology.

The Southern Jesus in Music and Holiness/Pentecostal Traditions

More than sermons, perhaps, gospel hymns introduced Jesus as friend to a post-Civil War generation of southerners. They portrayed Jesus with a human face—friendly, kindly, humble, and (usually) unmistakably fair, godly, pure, and white.

Black hymnists in the twentieth century took up the same themes, but eventually blackened them with counterimages of Jesus—much of this with the emergence of black Holiness/Pentecostalism in the South. Many of the early gospel bluesmen were associated with alternative and Holiness/Pentecostal religious groups. Arising in the late nineteenth century as a challenge to the evangelical religious establishment, Holiness/Pentecostal groups stressed the necessity of a second baptism, an infilling of the Holy Spirit, purifying the believer and consecrating him or her for service in this world. Pentecostals added to that a belief in speaking in tongues as a signifier of the seizure of the soul by the Holy Ghost. A whirlwind of religious groups spun out of the Holiness/Pentecostal movement. These new churches raised up scores of gospel bluesmen and blueswomen as well as legendary ministers and church entrepreneurs such as Charles Harrison Mason, founder of the Church of God in Christ. While the theology of the Holiness/Pentecostal groups focused on the movement of the Holy Ghost in the soul, their religious expressions often presented Jesus as an active presence in the world and in the believer's heart. Some groups, referred to as Oneness churches, held a theology that they referred to as "Jesus only." In their view, there was no Trinity because Jesus contained within himself Father, Son, and Holy Ghost.

Black Holiness and Oneness pioneer Charles Price Jones, a native of Mississippi and founder of the Church of Christ, Holiness, authored numerous editions of his own hymnal, *Jesus Only*, first published in 1899. As part of the Holiness movement of the late nineteenth century, Jones claimed entire sanctification in 1894. Then pastoring a Baptist church, he was "not satisfied with a faith that brought no fruit." He fasted three days and nights until "new visions of Christ, of God, of truth, were given me." Shortly after his conversion to Holiness, he wrote to a Baptist colleague: "It is so bad that we have not had faithful ministers with true and understanding hearts. . . . But in the name of Jesus we must now make a herculean effort to redeem the people."[35]

Charles Price Jones's herculean efforts included authoring almost one thousand hymns. One of his most popular was "Jesus Only," the lyrics revealed to him, as he later testified, when he reflected on his decision to leave the Baptist Church and found a religious movement more focused on Jesus's name. "It is the Name of Jesus alone that has salvation in it," he insisted, for "Christ must be all.

Holiness belongs to God. Christ is the life. All else is failure." The name of Jesus himself summoned spiritual authority and power, and Jones's hymns reflected the intense desire to see Him face to face:

> Then away with ev'ry idol,
> Let my Lord be all to me;
> Jesus only is my Master,
> Jesus only let me see.[36]

Jones originally had teamed with his compatriot in pioneering Holiness/Pentecostal teachings in Mississippi, Charles Harrison Mason, a native of Shelby County, Tennessee. While Mason was studying for the Baptist ministry in the 1890s, God showed him that "there was no salvation in schools and colleges," as he later wrote. Mason "arose and bade them a final farewell, to follow Jesus, with the Bible as my sacred guide." He received his Pentecostal conversion at the Azusa Street revivals in Los Angeles in 1906, and in the next two decades took that message through the South. Mason's preaching skill drew attention from blacks and whites alike. Church members and black Pentecostals generally recognized his special powers of discernment. Mason took the trunks of two saplings grown in the shapes of a hand and a foot (the former with five fingers, the latter with five toes), and gave them this interpretation: "It's God's time to cut off His children from worldliness setting them apart in His will baptized in the Christ mind." Criticized for bringing magic into the churches, he pointed to the scriptures, which indicated that Jesus practiced the same kinds of healings and spirit possessions that Mason himself preached.[37]

The liturgy of smaller Pentecostal denominations such as the Church of God, the Pillar and Ground of Truth, drew from the Pentecostal message but more explicitly blackened Jesus. In 1889, William Christian founded The Church of the Living God (Christian Workers for Fellowship) in Wrightsville, Arkansas, part of the growing Holiness movement. His catechism included the following call-and-response liturgy: "Was Jesus a member of the black race? Yes. Matthew I. How do you know? Because he was in the line of

Charles Harrison Mason, founder of the Church of God in Christ.
Courtesy of Sherry Sherrod Dupree.

Abraham and David the king. Is this assertion sufficient proof that Christ came of the black generation? Yes. Why? Because David said he became like a bottle in the smoke."³⁸

More so than theological treatises, antiquarian excavations of biblical stories to discover African characters, or metaphorically powerful literature of lynching victims as Christ figures, black southern song conveyed Christ images to believers. In the nineteenth century, spirituals profoundly captured the deepest yearnings of enslaved people. In the twentieth century, blues, gospel, freedom songs, and soul conveyed black life and theology.

The black southern Jesus of twentieth-century music grew directly from nineteenth-century traditions. Jesus as "leader" appeared frequently in antebellum song and sermon, and postbellum black Christians and artists picked up that theme. On one plantation in the 1870s, an Episcopalian missionary watched congregants led by a boy carrying a white banner with a red cross singing "We will march through the valley with faith; We will march through the valley of faith; and Jesus himself shall be our leader."³⁹ Some blues artists, traveling evangelists, and guitar men took up this imagery in their recordings in the early twentieth century. For example, the pioneering slide guitarist and sometime preacher Nehemiah "Skip" James, a native of a plantation near Jackson, Mississippi, put his ferocious guitar skills to use in "Jesus Is a Mighty Good Leader," a song recorded in 1931:

> Let Jesus lead you,
> Let Jesus lead you, all the way
> All the way from earth to heaven
> Let Jesus lead you, all the way
> He's a mighty good leader
> He's a mighty good leader, all the way
> All the way from earth to heaven
> He's a mighty good leader, all the way

The guitar tuning and sliding were innovative, but the song's sentiments drew from a familiar tradition of placing a very visible Jesus at the center of the spiritual quest. The repetition in the song structure and the communal nature of the "you" in the lyrics also characterized music from the era of the spirituals.[40]

From the 1920s to the 1950s, southern religious expression found an outlet on race discs that sometimes sold tens of thousands of copies. Jesus appears in manifold ways through these records. For example, William and Versey Smith's "Sinner You'll Need King Jesus" and Rev. Edward Clayborn's "This Time Another Year You May Be Gone" updated lyric scraps from older tunes and reproduced them on records aimed at a black audience and recorded in intense, blues-influenced styles. Luther Magby's "Jesus Is Getting Us Ready for That Great Day," employed a stringed band, brass instruments, and tambourines to back up his triumphant question, "And who shall be able to stand?"[41]

Gospel music often portrayed Jesus in gentler terms, forsaking the imagery of King Jesus as a warrior. Nonetheless, Jesus remained a central presence, one who would "take my hand" and lead weary travelers "through the storm, through the night," in the words of the gospel music classic "Precious Lord, Take My Hand." "I can pray, I can smile, I can feel Christ in me," gospel writers proclaimed, as they composed classics such as "Jesus Is All," "I'm Goin' to Bury Myself in Jesus's Arms," and "Jesus Will Make It Alright." The composers of the early gospel classics, notably Charles Albert Tindley, Lucie Campbell, and Thomas A. Dorsey, personalized Jesus, wove him into narratives of clearly delineated individual lives. In the early twentieth century, stories of Jesus taking one's hand, acting as comforter, leading one through trials and tribulations, assumed a central place. These are songs whose first-person narrative "I" recounts individual experiences, singing to a second-person "you" understood also to be an individual listener. In one of his earliest gospel recordings, Thomas Dorsey played and sang

> How well do I remember how Jesus brought me through?
> I prayed and walked the floor a night or two.
> I said, "Lord, take and use me, that's all that I can do."
> And I gave my heart to Jesus. How 'bout you?
> (Chorus)

> How 'bout you?
> I hope my Savior is your Savior too.
> I said "Lord, take and use me, that's all that I can do."
> And I gave my heart to Jesus, how 'bout you.

The B side of "How 'bout You," a record that essentially was the birth of black gospel music in commercial recording, was a classic soon to be taken up by gospel artists for the rest of the twentieth century: "If You See My Saviour." The words tell of "standin' by the bedside of a neighbor," waiting for his death and giving him a message to take to the other side:

> If you see my Savior, tell him that you saw me
> When you saw me I was on my way
> You may meet some old friend who may ask you for me
> Tell him I am coming home some day.[42]

Early blues and gospel pioneers, especially the street evangelists and bluesmen guitarists from Blind Lemon Jefferson to Washington Phillips, Blind Willie Johnson, and Charley Patton (who recorded his religious sides under the pseudonym Elder J. J. Hadley) and Sister Rosetta Tharpe, sang of Jesus accompanied by guitar licks that were unmistakably African American. In their southern song, Jesus appeared in multiple guises in everyday environments. He was a friend, a ticket taker at the depot, a railroad engineer, a passenger in a car, or an airplane pilot. Jesus transcended all denominational divisions in Washington Phillips's classic "Denomination Blues," which concluded "you better have Jesus, that's all." With the extension of railroads through the rural South, Jesus became indelibly associated with a train taking one to a better place. When one sharecropper began to "think seriously about the salvation of my soul," he saw himself at a train station, standing next to Jesus: "my knees got weak and I knelt to pray. As I knelt Jesus handed me a ticket. It was all signed with my name. I arose to my feet and handed it at the window and was told to take my place with the three men standing on the platform and wait." Ministers preached that sinful men were like passengers "who have purchased their tickets at the Calvary's union station stamped with the blood of Christ and the insignia of God to meet Christ the Lord." Artists such as Blind Lemon Jefferson sang of traveling by train across the Jordan River, fearing nothing because "Jesus gonna be my engineer." Gospel bluesman Henry Thomas would wait for Jesus at the train station: "I'll meet you at the station when the train come along," the smoke from the train indicating Jesus's arrival.[43]

In 1926, shortly before his own death, Blind Lemon Jefferson recorded some classic lines of southern "hard religion" in his tune "All I Want Is the Pure Religion, Hallelu," which features verses about how "death is ridin' all through the land" and how the train taking people from this "sinful world" had "done turned the curve." The final verse concludes:

> Ride on Death, don't ride so slow, hallelu, hallelu.
> Ride on Death, don't ride so slow, hallelu.
> Ride on Death, don't ride so slow, my heart's willing, ready to go.
> Sayin', you're gonna need that pure religion, hallelu, oh hallelu.

Jefferson's stark rendering of life came through clearly in his tune "Please See My Grave Is Kept Clean," which numerous white guitarists and singers also recorded. Following his early death, his fans compared him directly to Christ. Rev. Emmett Dickinson eulogized the guitarist this way:

> Let us pause for a moment
> And look at the life of our beloved Blind Lemon Jefferson who
>   was born blind
> It is in many respects like that of our Lord, Jesus Christ
> Like Him, unto the age of thirty he was unknown
> And also like Him in a short space of a little over three years
> His name and his works were known in every home.[44]

Through the twentieth century, Southern churches remained separated by race, and southern religious institutions explicitly segregated. Yet they shared common cultural frames of reference, expressed especially through music. Visions of Jesus among working class and rural southerners, too, ran parallel in the segregated institutions. This was a Jesus of a southern hard religion who was part savior and part trickster.

The rise of southern denominations to respectability and even cultural dominance tamed passions that had inspired their explosive growth in the early nineteenth century. A denominational gospel of uplift and internalized self-control pushed back older southern traditions of ecstatic visions and wild personal struggles with forces seen and unseen. This gospel of uplift made its way into the countryside, where black and white denominational leaders sought to inculcate respectable modes of living and worshipping. Ministers in the countryside urged their parishioners to make better homes. Rather than scraps of newspapers and catalogs on walls, they advised that "It is better and will prove more beneficial to the young to have on your walls a picture showing the arrest, crucifixion, burial, resurrection, and ascension of our Lord and Savior Jesus Christ."[45]

Working-class and rural southerners, who were increasingly pushed off their lands and from their livelihoods but not yet integrated into a New South bourgeois order, maintained a "hard religion," one that reflected powerfully the uncertainties and vagaries of their own lives. Besides the sentimental Jesus who appeared in so many gospel hymns and the ultimately triumphant Savior who populated black gospel hymnody, southern folk also gave voice to an unsparing Jesus who appeared only after great struggle and turmoil, most often in fleeting visionary experiences. Left behind by the dominant religious institutions, this southern Jesus remained a presence in the rural and working-class South.

For both white and black southern believers, this Jesus was involved with people in mortal combat with forces beyond their control. This Jesus came to people in moments of ecstasy and agony. He arrived mysteriously and in different guises and appeared to strugglers in dreams and visions. In folklore, visions, music, and in personal narratives, southerners encountered Jesus less as a "friend" than a guide who appeared sporadically, spontaneously, and unpredictably.[46]

In this southern working-class tradition, Jesus as savior was often not a vision of light, for rural sermons emphasized the "persecuted man who suffers violence." The followers of the man who courted and achieved violent death through blood also would be ridiculed, ignored by those who sought worldly pleasures. As one Kentucky coal miner and preacher said: "if you ain't got a blood bought religion you ain't got a thing in the world. . . . Because the Bible plainly tells us that Jesus Christ died on Calvary's cross and shed the last drop of his blood that through him, not through some church, not through some big fine house, not through some big fine school, not through some great big preacher, not through some other way, but the way that the Lord has laid down, the plan of salvation. . . . According to the blood, . . . the plan of salvation has always been the blood route." It was Jesus's death, not his resurrection, that preoccupied white southern working-class theology. Carlos Williams, rural white preacher in Wise County, Virginia, in 1939, felt that Jesus was not "just a spirit" but rather appeared

> as a man just like me
> and that's the reason he come into the world he was a kin to his people brethren there's a relationship there and I want you to know today that
> > if Jesus hadn't a been
> if he hadn't a been a man
> he wouldn't a cared nothing about the man
> and that's the reason he died for him
> and I want you to know he never died for just a spirit because he didn't
> > need to die for a spirit
> but the man is what Jesus had under consideration.[47]

As a humanly vulnerable man, Jesus comprehended the struggles of this world.

In black southern theology of this generation, Jesus appears as a man too—usually described with some variant of the phrase "little man" or "little white man"—but his symbology becomes much more complicated. Certainly the African Americans who recounted their conversion experiences for interviews later collected in *God Struck Me Dead* conjured memorable visions of Jesus. He was usually seen as a small white man, beckoning suffering souls to come over to the other side. Zora Neale Hurston, daughter of a Baptist minister, was a lifelong religious skeptic who knew intimately the shortcomings of the believers. Churchgoers in her all-black hometown lived entirely normal lives, she soon learned: "They plowed, chopped wood, went possum-hunting, washed clothes, raked up back yards and cooked collard greens like anybody else." Even with her doubts and questions, she felt moved in churches "not by the spirit, but by action, more or less dramatic." Candidates for membership were pursued by "hellhounds" as they "ran for salvation." They would dangle precariously over the fires of hell, call on Jesus, see a "little white man" on the other side, and finally traverse to heaven. In publicly describing their spiritual journeys, they sometimes strayed from the expected scripted narrative, relying instead on extemporaneously created variations: "These visions are traditional. I knew them by heart as did the rest of the congregation. Some of them made up new details. Some of them would forget a part and improvise clumsily or fill up the gap with shouting. The audience knew, but everybody acted as if every word of it was new."[48]

In another of Hurston's accounts, a black Baptist deacon saw himself chased by hellhounds, a penalty for his sins: "Then I saw myself hanging over hell by one strand of hair and de flames of fire leapin up a thousand miles to swaller my soul an I cried: 'Jesus, save my soul and I'll believe, I'll believe.' Then I found myself on solid ground and a tall white man beckoned for me to come to him and I went, wrapped in my guilt, and he 'noited me wid de oil of salvation and healed all my wounds." Pioneering black historian Carter Woodson heard similar testimonies in rural churches and recorded them in his 1930 work *The Rural Negro*. In his telling, converts described themselves lying prostrate, awakening from their "stupor," and crying out, "Thank God I was born to die!" Jesus had "snatched me like a brand from eternal burning," as one respondent related, "and saved me from hell's dark door." Woodson explained that "all the candidate needs to do is to convince the brethren that he had some such experience as they themselves had—that he saw a light, heard a voice, had a vision, outwitted the devil, or received a visit from Jesus. With such a straight story they find ready acceptance in the Church."[49]

Jesus's appearances in black literature set in the Jim Crow past suggest an undercurrent of skepticism about whether the white Jesus of American history ever could become the black Jesus of African American visions. In Alice Walker's *The Color Purple*, Celie's skeptical friend Shug tells her that the God preached in church is the one that is "in the white folks' Bible." Celie responds, "God wrote the Bible, white folks had nothing to do with it." Shug shoots back, "How come he look just like them, then? She say. Only bigger? And a heap more hair? How come the Bible just like everything else they make, all about them doing one thing and another, and all the colored folks doing is gitting cursed." Celie has no answer except, "I never thought about that." Similarly, in playwright August Wilson's signature work, *Joe Turner's Come and Gone*, black southern migrants who have settled in Pittsburgh connect Jesus Christ with a darker southern past: "Great big old white man . . . your Mr. Jesus Christ. Standing there with a whip in one hand and a tote board in another, and them niggers swimming in a sea of cotton."[50]

An undercurrent of skepticism about the utility of Christianity runs through black southern history—from the indifference of early eighteenth-century slaves to the Society for the Propagation of the Gospel in Foreign Parts, to the identification of bluesmen with a devil who was attractive to them, to black theologians who understood the consequences of Jesus's transformation into a figure of white power in American history.

Black bluesmen and blueswomen, gospel and secular, encouraged and sometimes expressed this same skepticism, and their work suggests much also about the emotional erotics of Jesus. The tensions and contradictions in their own lives arose from their struggle to balance the sacred and the profane. A generation of white southern artists in midcentury explored this same dangerous but enticing terrain. The hard religion, personal demons, and brilliantly recorded struggles of figures such as Hank Williams, Johnny Cash, Jerry Lee Lewis, and other white southerners of that generation arose from a legacy of working-class religion in the South that rejected the conventional southern denominational formulas. In their world, shouting and bodily ecstasy signified communion with and visions of Jesus.

Jesus was friend and savior in the gospel classics recorded by these legends. As a boy, Elvis Presley left his house one day, his Aunt Lorene recalled, and returned later, explaining that "he had been talking to Jesus." Later, in December 1956, just at the first zenith of his national stardom, Elvis sat down at the famous "Million-Dollar Sessions" together with Carl Perkins, Jerry Lee Lewis, and for a briefer time Johnny Cash. Relaxing after a day of recording, Elvis returned to his beloved gospel classics. At this 1956 session, he slowed down the snappy quartet tempo to record a meditative piece, "Just a Little Talk with Jesus." The tune had been penned by a black Tennessean, Cleavant Derricks, whose gospel catalogue was taken up enthusiastically by early white country and rock 'n' roll singers from Bill Monroe to George Jones to Elvis Presley. The Stamps-Baxter Company, a white gospel music company and publishing powerhouse, distributed Derricks's songs widely among white southern gospel singers; the same company took black gospel songs and popularized them among whites. "Just a Little Talk with Jesus" goes through the evangelical story of being "lost in sin" before "Jesus took me in," with a "little light from heaven" filling the singer's soul. As the song concludes, Jesus "is a friend who watches day and night"; during times of strife, "just a little talk with Jesus gonna make it right."[51]

But Jesus was not present or visible enough to forestall descents into self-destruction or the impulse to enjoy the pleasures of the flesh. Hank Williams's recording of "I Saw the Light" suggests the power of the divine light: "Then Jesus came like a stranger in the night / Praise the Lord, I saw the light." But it was not so easy as that. At the time of that recording, Hank Williams was but a few years from an early death, unlike Johnny Cash, who survived his demonic obsessions with pills and suicidal thoughts. Stories of Hank's last days interpreted the tragedy in appropriately mythical terms. The best-known legend portraying his presentiment of an early end has him drunkenly singing "I Saw the Light" at a concert with Minnie Pearl and saying that "There ain't no light." For him, it was all dark.

Both the more sentimental music of southern evangelicalism and the tunes of southern hard religion come through in the career of Johnny Cash. The persona of the man in black embodied a darkness symbolizing both his own Christ-like identification with the poor and downtrodden in society and his constant struggle with personal demons. His internal battle was between his own desires for piety and his manic pursuits. In the midst of recording classics such as *Johnny Cash at Folsom Prison* and later a similar piece at San Quentin, Cash managed to travel to the holy land and film a biographical rendering of Jesus's life, *The Gospel Road: The Story of Jesus*. In the film, as Cash delivers the narrative of Jesus's life with his signature style of rhythmic storytelling and guitar strumming, the character of Jesus, portrayed by a very Norwegian-looking Robert Elfstrom, strides through the holy land in robes of white, with a long shock of blond hair dazzling disciples and followers alike. A piece reflecting on his making of *The Gospel Road* suggested that

> In pre-dating Mel Gibson's *The Passion of the Christ*, Cash focused on Jesus' life and impact and resurrection, rather than the circumstances of his death. Although, fascinatingly, *The Gospel Road* depicted Jesus' crucifixion—albeit briefly—first in the desert and then inserted into the fleshpots of New York, Las Vegas and Hollywood. "This picture is relevant in New York City also," Cash told the *Times*. "At the end we show Christ dying on the cross in the desert. Then we show him dying in the same way with backdrops in New York, Las Vegas and Hollywood. Christ is real to me everywhere."[52]

With his wife, June Carter Cash, playing Mary Magdalene, Cash's life of Jesus spread through evangelical communities. Cash was the man in black (he remained adorned in his trademark black even in *The Gospel Road*) who had given himself over to a man bathed in white. As Cash put it, "I've lived all my life for the devil up 'til now, and from here on I'm going to live it for the Lord." With salvation by Jesus and the loving hand of June Carter Cash and a Christian community, Cash hoped to have the "kingdom of God building inside you and growing." Less than a decade later,

Cash's much less publicized struggles with alcohol and with suicidal thoughts showed that he was still chasing a dragon that appeared to him in blackness. Cash's recordings follow a trajectory well known to southerners, and especially to bluesmen, as they struggled within themselves between sacred and profane impulses.[53]

Cash's recordings toward the end of his life, collected in a five-volume *American Recordings* set, allowed him ample space to explore his lifelong mutually contradictory passions. In his music, Jesus appears as a figure of lightness and grace, but "the beast in me," when he became a trickster figure, was more than powerful enough to overcome and simply snuff out Jesus's presence on earth. "The beast in me," Johnny Cash sang, "is caged by frail and fragile bars." Cash's exploration of characters experiencing a dark night of the soul recurred through his musical career (so much so that other songwriters produced works such as "Beast in Me" specifically for Cash to record); his periodic reversion to a more triumphalist Christ could not overcome Cash's own attraction to songs about the mortal struggle for the soul. His later music expressed intense struggles with Jesus. In "Redemption," Cash summed up a lifetime of hard living and expressed an older culture of a hard religion. From the hands, side, and feet of Jesus, the blood "came down," and where "a teardrop fell in the deep crimson dew / the tree of life grew."

Jesus's blood watered the tree, which bore fruit, feeding the singer. Even when "Lucifer came" to keep him in chains, the singer saw through the trickster of the "six-sixty-six." The singer concludes the elaborate metaphor by hearing an inner voice insisting "'You do have a choice,'" and "the vine engrafted me / And I clung to the tree."

Very late in his life, Cash sang somewhat menacingly of "your own, personal Jesus," one who would be there even when "you're all alone / flesh and bone / by the telephone," waiting to receive the call from the deliverer. Cash's classic recordings in *Man in Black* and his haunting *American Recordings* captured his conflicted soul and his background in rural Arkansas, where, in the words of Billy Joe Shaver, "Jesus Was Our Savior—Cotton Was Our King."[54]

Cash carried forward a tradition that both white and black

artists had sung about through the middle years of the twentieth century. It found expression from pioneering bluesman Charley Patton's "Prayer of Death" (from the early 1930s) to Cash's own "Redemption" and "Personal Jesus." This was a personal Jesus of suffering southerners from both sides of the color line. Ultimately, this Jesus was too subversive to be segregated.

The ambiguity of Jesus makes him a perfect symbol for the paradoxes and contradictions of southern history and also a figure who can heal the wounds of the divisions created by that history. In the civil rights era, in particular, Jesus's previously more submerged black sympathies emerged dramatically. American religious thought and imagery would never be the same.

Everybody Always Talking Black Jesus

Looking at the sociological literature produced in the 1930s and 1940s, including Benjamin Mays's *The Negro's God, as Reflected in His Literature* and E. Franklin Frazier's *Negro Youth at the Crossways: Their Personality Development in the Middle States*, few would have predicted any revolutionary transformation of the southern white Christ into the black civil rights Jesus. Images of whiteness, Frazier and others found, dominated and warped the minds of black churchgoers, providing a divine imprimatur for the unjust social order. If God appeared as a white man, then the white man might be all powerful. But what Frazier did not see was that the youth who responded to his surveys were ambiguous about Jesus's color or race and often held sophisticated views about how Jesus's white imagery could be manipulated. As they saw it, Jesus was "white but not really white." They perceived that Jesus's race was socially constructed and thus could be reconstructed.[55]

Activists in the civil rights era, and the proponents of black theology, understood themselves to be reimagining, and reimaging, God and Christ. Theirs was a theological project argued out in formal treatises. But images of a black Jesus, as we have seen, could be heard and seen in black music and arts through the twentieth century. In alternative black religious institutions, literary expression, and in some examples of African American religious art, Jesus broke out of a straitjacket of an invisible but very real whiteness. Perhaps people instinctively understood that a powerful divine would necessarily be a personal divine, one imagined in ways that made sense in everyday life. As black artists and writers and musicians challenged the white Jesus so dominant in southern culture, the roots of a Jesus of the civil rights movement emerged. Then in the 1950s and 1960s, he exploded, much to the surprise of many theological elites.

Black theologians from the nineteenth century forward had understood that the white God damaged black aspirations. The theological and psychological studies (especially Frazier's) of the interwar years reinforced this view. The critique of God/Jesus as white, for example, ran through black humanist and theologian Howard Thurman's penetrating *Jesus and the Disinherited*, a short explanation of Christianity's appeal to the oppressed. The accepted behavior patterns of the South, he suggested, assumed

> segregation to be normal—if normal, then correct; if correct, then moral; if moral, then religious. . . . God, for all practical purposes, is imaged as an elderly, benign white man, seated on a white throne, with bright, white light emanating from his countenance. Angels are blond and brunets suspended in the air around his throne to be his messengers and execute his purposes. Satan is viewed as being red with the glow of fire. But the imps, the messengers of the devil, are black. . . . The implications of such a view are simply fantastic in the intensity of their tragedy. Doomed on earth to a fixed and unremitting status of inferiority, of which segregation is symbolic, and at the same time cut off from the hope that the Creator intended it otherwise, those who are thus victimized are stripped of all social protection. . . . Under such circumstances, there is but a step from being despised to despising oneself.[56]

A generation later, black theology pushed these insights further. Whereas Thurman's generation would have preferred to deracialize Christ, to remove his whiteness but not replace it with blackness, the theological generation of the 1960s perceived imparting blackness (whether physically or metaphorically) on the divine as a necessary instrument of liberation.

Black theology did not invent or create notions of a black Jesus or God, for this was a long-running tradition in African American song, sermon, art, folktale, and imagery. Through the first half of the twentieth century, texts by self-taught theological authors as well as literati such as Countee Cullen and Du Bois portrayed Jesus as black. The gospel blues and the powerfully idiosyncratic music from the recordings done in the interwar years blackened Jesus in sound. The trumpet, the tambourine, the drum, and the blue note heralded the appearance of the Savior and provided the soundtrack for American popular religious music.

Black artists took up the complex question of representing Jesus in a culture that worshipped the Jesus shown in the ubiquitous prints of Warner Sallman's painting *Head of Christ*, whose face *was* Jesus for many people. Regardless of the imagery invoked, Jesus represented blackness in an existential sense of standing in for suffering humanity. This notion, drawn from a wide variety of nineteenth-century work, grew more literal in the twentieth century as the imagery itself darkened. Black theology codified this movement, but it did not invent it.

According to art historian Jennifer Strychasz, black religious imagery of the period before black theology "engaged in a complex negotiation between assimilation into the dominant white Christian framework and the desire to assert an African American identity."[57] For example, Lemuel Graham's *The Gospel Train*, unveiled in 1948 in a black Methodist church in Maryland, featured a modern red, white, and blue striped train in a rural setting. Graham drew from the deep train imagery in African American song, sermon, and art, including the well-known sermon "Black Diamond Express to Hell" and accompanying diagram "Two Railroads to Eternity." He also might have borrowed from William Gates's *Little Black Train Is Coming*, one of the most popular recorded sermons of the 1920s and a work fraught with African American train symbolism of segregation, deliverance, and freedom. In black sermon and song, as well as in this painting, the train took passengers from unenlightened ignorance to personal deliverance, from southern enslavement to northern freedom. On these trains, Jesus took tickets, ran the locomotive, and shepherded people safely into the depot. The painting incorporated narratives of slavery, race, and redemption in a religious context. While the figures in the painting may have been white, the unambiguous symbolism resonated with African American influences.[58]

Alternate images of Jesus run through the work of trained as well as self-taught black and white southern artists through the twentieth century. In his 1939 work *Jesus and the Three Marys*, South Carolina native William H. Johnson (1901–1970) constructed a narrative of a fervent faith based on evangelical traditions of southern African Americans. Johnson depicted a black crucified Jesus (who is also something of a self-portrait of the artist as a young man) raised on the cross in the center, with a dark-skinned Mary Magdalene and Mary, sister of Martha, underneath, reaching up to him in Holiness/Pentecostal fashion. Elongated arms and exaggeratedly large hands, painting techniques straight from the modernist and surrealist traditions, dominate the center of the canvas and reflect Johnson's studies in Denmark and Scandinavia in the years before he tackled his best-known work. While influenced by the European artistic tradition of rendering the crucifixion, Johnson transformed his work into an encounter with the "primitive" both in the artistic primitivist sense as well as the "primitive" as applied to African Americans. Johnson wanted viewers to internalize a black Jesus through observing the expressions of churchgoing black folk. While Picasso and others searched for African masks and Pacific Island totems for inspiration, "Johnson's primitivism turned inward, focusing on a self defined by racial difference, cultural distinctiveness, a marginal status in society, and an identification with black . . . spirituality."[59]

The work of these self-taught artists resulted from personal experience rendered through an imaginative artistic lens. The vernacular artists often placed Christ in a vivid millennialist framework, alongside Daniel, Ezekiel, and characters from the Book of Revelation, or in artistic settings suggesting how his suffering paralleled that

William L. Johnson, *Jesus and the Three Marys*, 1939.
Courtesy of the Gallery of Art, Howard University.

of African Americans. For example, the self-taught Clementine Hunter, a native of Louisiana, mixed the Catholic influences of her state with the reigning Protestantism of the region in works such as *Black Jesus, On a Cross with Figures, White Flowers, and Birds*. Similarly in *Crucifixion with Red Zinnias*, the long-lived Louisianan showed that black Jesus images would not have to wait for a specific theology that made more ideological claims for their merit.

Working her way up from a childhood on a plantation and through many years in Natchitoches, Hunter developed her own personal, vivid imagery that naturally placed Jesus in a context that spoke to her individually. "Everybody always talking Black Jesus," she responded when asked why she started her series of crucified black Jesus paintings (scenes often set against lighter pastel colors, flowers, and birds) in the 1940s. One of them, *Black Christ on a Cross*, envisions black angels in white robes symbolically lifting the crucified black Christ to heaven.

Eventually, Hunter produced over one hundred such works. One of them in particular, *Cotton Crucifixion*, paralleled the tradition in black song and literature of identifying black suffering with Christ's appearance in the contemporary world. Like most self-taught southern religious artists, Hunter viewed her works not as products to sell but as fulfillments of divine commandments to render artistically her personal religious visions.[60]

Black Jesus figures appear frequently in mid-twentieth century southern self-taught art, including works from artists such as Bill Traylor, Elijah Pierce, and Anderson Johnson. The work of Johnson, currently being enshrined in his own museum in Newport News, Virginia, suggests that these artists' spiritually based motivations compelled them in directions that later would become formalized and systematized in theology. Johnson was a native of Virginia and former assistant to Daddy Grace in the United Church of Prayer for all People. After settling in Newport News, and building his own Faith Mission there, Johnson spent his career stuffing his church with his own artistic images. One of his best-known images, *Behold the Man*, presents a closeup of Jesus almost jumping off the canvas

Clementine Hunter, *Crucifixion with Red Zinnias*, 1965.
Oil on canvas, 24" × 18", Collection of Ann and Jack Brittain and their Children.

Black Christ on Cross. Clementine Hunter (1886/87–1988), Natchitoches, Louisiana, 1972. Oil on Cardboard. 27¼" × 12¼". Collection American Folk Art Museum, New York. Gift of Mrs. Chauncey Newlin. 1991.23.1. Photographed by Gavin Ashworth, New York.

Clementine Hunter, *Cotton Crucifixion*, 1970.
Oil on masonite, 27" × 19", collection of Gordon W. Bailey.

Anderson Johnson, *Behold the Man*. Courtesy of the Georgia Museum of Art, Collection of Carl and Marian Mullis.

at the viewer, black eyes and beard set off sharply against a green background.[61]

New Orleans native Gertrude Morgan also expressed the common view that she had been directly commanded to produce art for her faith. In her self-portrait titled *Canty*, done probably in the mid-1960s, Morgan adopts a formal black dress and a white collar, showing herself a missionary for the church and also preparing for her marriage to Jesus Christ. She is set against a backdrop of devotional words, including "I am very happy for who I am the Bride of Jesus Christ." In other works, including *Self-Portrait in White With Jesus*, Morgan experimented with alternative and experimental artistic forms. *Self-Portrait in White with Jesus*, for example, is a collage pasted onto a guitar case that she used in her evangelizing efforts. The work furthers her vision of being the bride of Christ and also artistically portrays her own conception of her decades-long ministry of preaching, playing music, and producing art.[62]

In Miami-born Purvis Young's *Black Jesus*, 1974, a black and ponytailed crucified Jesus dominates the front of the painting against a busy mural of objects in the background. A tear coming from Jesus's eye comments on the action swirling around him and directly encounters the viewer.

In addition to paintings, murals, and other works from both fine and self-taught artists, southern literature has grappled with the figure of Jesus. America's God was white, and suggestions otherwise raised provocative challenges. Literary figures seized them, for Jesus's racial ambiguity in a region full of evangelical religion and violent bloodlust made for compelling stories. Du Bois did so repeatedly. Less frequently but at much greater length, so did William Faulkner. In Faulkner's *Light in August*, Joe Christmas parallels Jesus's life in numerous ways, from his obscure parentage to his appearing in town on Christmas day and finally to his virtual lynching at the age of thirty-three. As a black man who could pass for white but chose not to, Christmas seems to play upon the ambiguity of the southern Christ image—again, as the black teenager had told interviewers for E. Franklin Frazier in the 1930s, Jesus was "white but not really white."

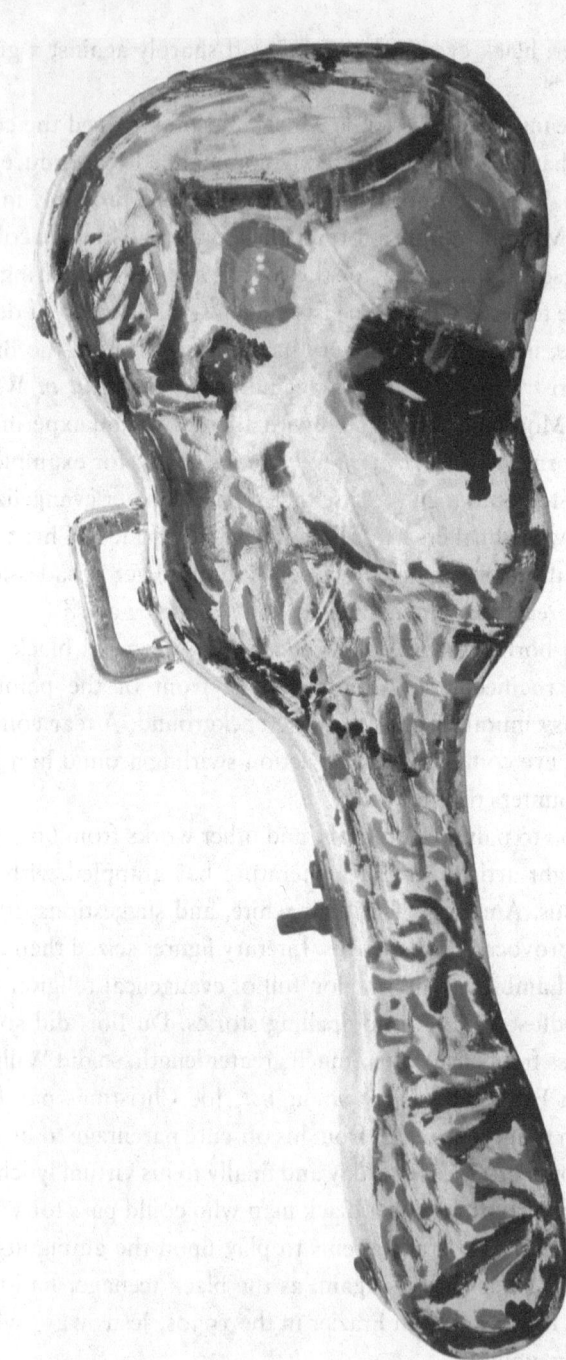

Sister Gertrude Morgan, *Self-Portrait in White With Jesus*.
Courtesy of Ben Jaffe and the Jaffe Family Collection, New Orleans.

Purvis Young, *Black Jesus*. From the 1974 installation *Goodbread Alley*. Courtesy Skot Foreman Fine Art, www.skotforeman.com.

John Henrik Clarke's story from this era, "The Boy Who Painted Christ Black," also captures Christ's racial ambiguity and shows how even a potential of blackness could threaten a world beholden to the white Christ. In the story, Aaron Crawford, a boy in a fictional school in Muskogee County, Georgia, found that he had artistic talents and used them to paint a "large picture of Christ—painted black!" The boy's uncle, who taught Negro history classes at the YMCA, had said black folks were the "most powerful on earth. When I asked him about Christ, he said no one ever proved whether he was black or white." This was the genesis of the picture: "Somehow a feeling came over me that he was a black man, 'cause he was so kind and forgiving, kinder than I have ever seen white people be. So, when I painted this picture I couldn't help but paint it as I thought it was." Aaron's picture, moreover, "looked much different from the one I saw hanging on the wall when I was in Sunday School. It looked more like a helpless Negro, pleading silently for mercy," rather than the familiar *Head of Christ* painting that it probably replaced. When the school superintendent came to lecture the children about Booker T. Washington, he saw Aaron Crawford's picture of Christ and took offense. He asked, "Who painted this sacrireligious nonsense." Aaron responded that he did, adding that blacks had as much right to paint Jesus as colored as whites had to paint him white. The schoolteacher had encouraged him, noting that artists targeted particular audiences with their messages, the same point hammered home by Henry McNeal Turner through the late nineteenth century. And it made some historic sense to paint Christ black, for "Christ was born in that part of the world that had always been predominantly populated by colored people." Quite possibly, then, Christ was a Negro, the principal had assured them. The principal reinforced the message that blacks had been creators of civilization. But the superintendent of the school warned, "There'll be a lot of fuss in this world if you start people thinking that Christ was a nigger." He reprimanded the boy, removed him from the school, and fired the principal.[63]

The ambiguity of the place and race of Jesus for black southerners engendered multiple responses. In some cases, it spurred a rejection of the Christian tradition, or at least a suspicion of it. For instance, in 1963 Mississippian Anne Moody was gripped by the feeling that God was white and that she hated Him. In other cases, it encouraged black theologians from Henry McNeal Turner to James Cone to reenvision Christ in the image of African Americans. This feeling motivated Martin Luther King's generation to overcome the religious sanctioning of white supremacist power.

Mind Stayed on Jesus, and on Freedom

Entering the era of the modern civil rights movement, African Americans had inherited contending images of Jesus as subversive savior and as the living representative of the white man's God. Overcoming the racialization of the divine proved an emotionally fraught struggle for many during the years of the civil rights revolution. The conflicting imagery could be seen on the walls of countless black churches and homes, where Sallman's *Head of Christ* as well as white political heroes mixed with images from icons of black history. Jesus was a comforter to the afflicted but could be a salve that took a generation's eyes off the prize. The critique from the black secular left as well as from Black Muslims condemned as hopelessly outdated those who would sing, "You may have all the world, but give me Jesus." With minds "stayed on Jesus," could minds be focused on freedom? Then too, Jesus could be an avenger, the one calling the chickens home to roost. The black appropriation of the southern evangelical Christ, and his reemergence as the white Christ of southern racial power, clashed in the twentieth century. For African Americans, Jesus had to be saved. Doing so involved a reimagination of the same evangelical culture of salvation and segregation that was part of his creation.

The centuries-long interplay between a universal Savior and a racially defined Jesus came to a head in the twentieth-century South. The imagery of the black artists, the poetry and stories of the black literati, and increasingly in theology, black Christianity resurrected this Jesus of the disinherited. Reflecting on the meaning of spirituals and freedom songs, Martin Luther King's colleague Joseph Lowery later recalled the "hypocrisy of faith" that surrounded black southerners. The fault lay "not with the religion, but with those who were practicing it. And they adopted the religion, and Jesus became a symbol of freedom and liberty. And the gospel to them was a liberating gospel. . . . And they figured that God was gonna deliver them." King learned similar lessons during his student years at Morehouse College. In 1945, his teacher George D. Kelsey began annual ministerial institutes aimed at educating black Baptist preachers. "I made it my business to present lectures on the most strenuous teaching of Jesus," Kelsey later recalled. "It was precisely at this time that Martin's eyes lit up most and his face was graced with a smile."[64]

Sitting in his kitchen during the evening of January 27, 1956, not yet two months into the Montgomery bus boycott, Martin Luther King was overcome with a vision, a transcendent moment that steeled him for the difficult days to come. Discouraged by constant threats and setbacks, King pondered giving up leadership of the nascent movement, which was to consume the next year of his life. Early negotiations with the city of Montgomery had soured, and he feared for the safety of his family. Having withstood dozens of threatening phone calls, that January evening he felt depleted. Then another phone call came around midnight. A threatening voice growled, "Nigger, we are tired of you and your mess now, and if you aren't out of this town in three days, we're going to blow your brains out and blow up your house." King realized the burden was on him alone. He had to

> call on that something in that person that your Daddy used to tell you about, that power that can make a way out of no way. And I discovered then that religion had become real to me, and I had to know God for myself. And I bowed down over that cup of coffee. I will never forget it . . . I prayed a prayer, and I prayed out loud that night. I said, "Lord, I'm down here trying to do what's right. I think I'm right. I think the cause that we represent is right. But Lord, I must confess that I'm weak now. I'm faltering. I'm losing my courage. And I can't let the people see me like this because if they see me weak and losing my courage, they will begin to get weak."

Then he sensed a voice commanding him to "stand up for righteousness. Stand up for justice. Stand up for truth. And lo I will be with you, even until the end of the world." He heard the "voice of Jesus saying still to fight on. He promised never to leave me, never to leave me alone." His fears diminished, and his "uncertainty disappeared." Just three days later, when local whites tried to destroy his home, King emerged unscathed, calmed an angry crowd, and urged the discipline of Christian love and nonviolence even in the face of such attacks. His encounter with the spirit of God, in the voice of Jesus, had settled in him.[65]

A vision of Jesus in a civil rights conversion experience had given King strength to love. "Love is the only way. Jesus discovered that," he told an audience in 1957 while reflecting on the power of nonviolence to overcome the violence of the segregationist state. "Yes, I can see Jesus walking around the hills and the valleys of Palestine. And I can see him looking out at the Roman Empire with all of her fascinating and intricate military machinery." He could hear Jesus rejecting the use of violence, and he urged his audience to march as Jesus did, even in the face of potential martyrdom. Answering the question of whether King's martyrdom was foreordained, Benjamin Mays, the "schoolmaster of the movement" who was King's teacher at Morehouse, answered that it was inevitable, not because God willed it, but "Inevitable in that any man who takes the position that King did . . . if he persists in that long enough, he'll get killed. Now. Anytime. That was the chief trouble with Jesus: He was a troublemaker."[66]

"The whole spirit of nonviolence came to me from Jesus of Nazareth," King explained.[67] But while Jesus taught the spirit, Gandhi had captured the technique of putting the spirit into action. More than anyone else, Gandhi took the "love ethic of Jesus Christ and made it effective as a sociopolitical force and brought about the transformation of a great nation and achieved freedom for his people."[68] From his study of Gandhi, King had learned that nonviolence could be an "effective and powerful social force on a large scale," not merely limited to individual social relations. King soon came to see that the "Christian doctrine of love operating through the Gandhian method of nonviolence was one of the most potent weapons available to the Negro in his struggle for freedom."[69]

King took those messages into his powerful exhortations to his congregants and fellow bus boycotters in Montgomery. At the beginning of the boycott, during a December 5, 1955, rally at the Holt Street Baptist Church, he told a cheering crowd, "If we are wrong, God Almighty is wrong. If we are wrong, Jesus of Nazareth was merely a utopian dreamer and never came down to earth. If we are wrong, justice is a lie." He underscored the way a renewed and revitalized Christianity empowered the movement: "'We are a Christian people. We believe in the Christian religion. We believe in the teachings of Jesus. The only weapon that we have in our hands this evening is the weapon of protest." After the bombing of his home, he calmed a crowd with the words of Jesus: "He who lives by the sword will perish by the Sword." He told them to love their white brothers, as Jesus said love your enemies.[70] After the media and the attention had left Montgomery, King kept preaching a message of "Christ Our Starting Point." In a Sunday sermon from December 1958, for example, he suggests that it must be Christ, not God, that is the starting point for Christianity. While some might say that God is the starting point, nonetheless it remains true that "Christ [tells] us what God is like. God is Christlike. . . . Christ is the moral and spiritual ultimate."[71]

King identified with "bearing the cross," and seemed to recognize his own coming crucifixion. "When I took up the cross," he later said, "I recognized its meaning. The cross is something that you bear and ultimately that you die on."[72] Congregants responded by identifying King as their Christ figure. In 1956, a "white friend" told Martin Luther King Jr. that although the White Citizens' Council would meet that night, "they can't make you ride and you are not breaking any law, so continue in the spirit of Christ. He is your real leader." A "fellow Suffer" from the Sixteenth Street Baptist Church in Birmingham wrote that black mothers had "prayed that God would send us a leader such as you are. Now that the Almighty has regarded our lowly estate and has raised *you* among us." Recalling the 1960 student sit-ins in Nashville, John Lewis recited the rules:

"Don't talk back. Sit straight up. Don't laugh out. Don't curse. And at the end of the rules, it said something like 'Remember the teachings of Jesus, Gandhi, Martin Luther King.'"[73]

In the civil rights years, activists, theologians, artists, and intellectuals mounted a multifaceted assault against the white God. Segregation had been sanctified, and its defense thus concerned the preservation of purity. For that reason, the closer desegregation moved to the world of the private and intimate, the more difficult and contentious it became. Streetcars or buses in Montgomery were one thing; schools were another. Bus terminals were one thing; marriage laws another. Southern religious leaders historically had preached a divine who called believers to tend to their private worlds. The doctrine of the "Spirituality of the church," articulated with particular cogency by James Henley Thornwell in the nineteenth century, forbade any direct religious assault on the social order. But it did not forbid a righteous defense of the existing order.

The defense of private segregation, including the whiteness of those at the dinner table and the church pew, was about not being forced to go "into the intimate things where we don't want to go," as the pastor of the largest Protestant congregation in America, the First Baptist Church of Dallas, Texas, had said in the 1950s before the South Carolina legislature. W. A. Criswell's words signified the widespread view that Jesus required a pure people, and of course miscegenation bodily threatened that purity. "It was through sex that segregation attained cosmological significance," historian Jane Dailey has written, and this cosmological significance derived from views heightened during the Civil War and preached for decades afterward. The white Christ of American history thus was privatized, drawn into a defense of home, parish boundaries, and Christian academies educating white children in the post-Brown era.[74]

White southern believers defended the purity of their churches, and of their bodies, symbolized by Jesus's blood on the cross. In the most "moderate" versions, this was a silent endorsement of religious segregation via the hallowed doctrine of the spirituality of the church. In Jackson, Mississippi, Governor Ross Barnett attended the church pastored by Douglas Hudgins, the fastidious pastor of the state capital's First Baptist Church. Aptly called by one historian the "theologian of a closed society," Hudgins articulated a pristine view of the soul's competency before God, the purity of a salvation enacted outside the social world. Some fellow Baptists provided more pointed language to accompany Hudgins's politely silent endorsement of segregationism. One of his deacons outlined the commonly held view that "the facts of history make it plain that the development of civilization and of Christianity itself has rested in the hands of the white race." In the most extreme versions, belief in Christ compelled religious violence in defense of his word. Sam Bowers, the Laurel, Mississippi, resident who revived the state's White Knights of the Ku Klux Klan, intoned that "a Solemn, determined Spirit of Christian Reverence must be stimulated in all members." What other white residents called the "invasion" of Mississippi by civil rights workers, he referred to as the "crucifixion" of the state. The "empirical fact" of Christ's resurrection, he believed, meant that "the disciple has no alternative but to strive towards that great day when all Christ's enemies will be put under his feet." Jesus Christ himself had called Bowers to his "priestly task of preserving the purity of his blood and soil."[75]

While white supremacists defended Jesus as "the original segregationist" and pointed to scriptural sanction for the South's peculiar institutions, figures such as Vernon Johns and Martin Luther King preached that Jesus would judge the sins of the South. Vernon Johns did so directly before a group of white and black Baptist preachers at a joint session in 1960. During the tense and stilted meeting, Johns sat uncomfortably through the first sermon of a white minister, which focused on being washed in the blood of the Lamb. When his turn came, Johns directly preached out his anger about how religion undergirded the southern social order. "The thing that disappoints me about the Southern white church is that it spends all of its time dealing with Jesus after the cross, instead of dealing with Jesus before the cross," he told the ministers, who responded in nervous silence. The white South preached about the death of Jesus, not his life: "You don't hear so much about his three years of teaching that man's religion is revealed in the love of his fellow man. He who says he loves God and hates his fellow man is a liar, and the truth is not in him. That is what offended the leaders of Jesus' own established church as well as the colonial authorities from Rome. That's why they put him up there." Johns concluded with this admonition: "I want you to deal with Jesus before the cross. I don't give a damn what happened to him after the cross."[76]

Integrationist Christians denounced segregationists for poisoning and polluting the body of Jesus. "The Church is first of all the body of Christ, and in that Body we are one, not races or clans," declared a white Mississippi Methodist minister. Martin Luther King agreed: The "church is the Body of Christ. So when the church is true to its nature it knows neither division nor disunity. I am disturbed about what you [segregationists] are doing to the Body of Christ." The "beloved community," as King explained on another occasion, had to be integrated because "segregation is a blatant denial of the unity which we all have in Christ Jesus."[77]

King, Jesus, and Ambiguity of the Civil Rights Jesus

> Way down yonder in the graveyard walk
> I thank God I'm free at last
> Me and my Jesus going to meet and talk
> I thank God I'm free at last . . .
> Some of these mornings, bright and fair
> I thank God I'm free at last
> Goin' meet King Jesus in the air
> I thank God I'm free at last

When Martin Luther King Jr. exclaimed, "Thank God almighty, I'm free at last," at the March on Washington on August 28, 1963, a dream deeply rooted not only in the American dream but in African American religious history and culture seemed to be at a moment of culmination. It was not yet a moment of fulfillment, as King searingly noted in his address. The "old Negro spiritual" referenced by King at this zenith moment of the civil rights movement centrally featured encountering Christ. Jesus was a very personal being whom one would meet on earth and in heaven, face to face. He was a physical, not merely a spiritual, presence, and civil rights leaders had enlisted Him in their cause.

The very image of Jesus could signify the depth of the struggle to determine whether blacks could identify with the divine. On a Sunday morning just a little over two weeks after King's sermon to the nation, a group of nearly thirty black children sat in a basement of the Sixteenth Street Baptist Church in Birmingham, Alabama, awaiting the closing prayers of a sermon titled "The Love That Forgives." Upstairs, adult black congregants gathered for the upcoming service. They had seen a lot over the last several months. From March, when local minister Fred Shuttlesworth had convinced Martin Luther King and the Southern Christian Leadership Conference to come to town, the city had entered the forefront of the civil rights arena. During that spring, as television cameras rolled, civil rights protestors on the streets of Birmingham picketed. Eventually school children filled the jail cells of the tough industrial town, which had well earned its derisive appellation, "Bombingham." Martin Luther King had been arrested in April, and on April 16 he issued a masterful public letter from the jail explaining the motivations behind the movement. Repeatedly in his "Letter from a Birmingham Jail," he defended civil rights leaders from charges of being "extremists" by pointing to the facts that Jesus was an "extremist for love" and that the Apostle Paul had written from his jail cell that he bore on his body the marks of Christ. "Will we be extremists for the preservation of injustice or for the extension of justice?" King had asked. In his "Letter from a Birmingham Jail," as in the "I Have a Dream" speech, the figure of Jesus provided a potent symbol for the highest aspirations of the movement. The black Christ, the suffering servant who identified with the oppressed, had been reclaimed.

The evening before the morning service at the Sixteenth Street Baptist Church in Birmingham on September 15, 1963, a group of men from the United Klans of America set over one hundred sticks of dynamite outside the church, ready to release during Sunday worship. At about 10:20 a.m., the explosives destroyed the rear wall and steps of the church and blew out all but one of the stained glass windows. The surviving window frame had featured a stained glass rendering of Jesus leading the children, an image the more poignant since that Sunday had been "Youth Day" at the church. Although the frame and structure of the window miraculously survived, the window itself sustained damage: the face of Jesus had been blown off. In a gruesome parallel, one of the four girls killed in the bombing had been decapitated by bricks that fell into the basement room where the children had been dressing for the upcoming service.

In his eulogy for the murdered children, Martin Luther King explained again how their "unmerited suffering" would be "redemptive." Once again, Christ's black sympathies, his identification with the suffering of the oppressed, redeemed social orders that seemed irredeemably evil. And the way that suffering innocents melded with Jesus in imagery provided moral lessons for the ages. As King intoned at their funeral, the explosion that took the head of Jesus and the head of one of the girls also would destroy politicians who had fed their constituents with the "stale bread of hatred and the spoiled meat of racism." The blast also condemned "every Negro . . . who has passively accepted the evil system of segregation and who has stood on the sidelines in a mighty struggle for justice." The bombing showed that "we must be concerned not merely about who murdered them, but about the system, the way of life, the philosophy which produced the murderers."[78]

As King came to a systemic understanding of social evil, Mississippi's activists articulated a liberation theology forged not from formal study but from an everyday identification with Jesus. No one better exemplified the way Jesus personalized the civil rights struggle than Fannie Lou Hamer, the liberation theologian of the Mississippi Delta. Hamer's political stance required spiritual sustenance. As she told one group of black Mississippians, "we are tired of being mistreated. God wants us to take a stand. We can stand by registering to vote—go to the court to register to vote." Christ would side with the sharecroppers in Mississippi during their struggle. Answering the inevitable charges that civil rights workers were agitators and communists, she retorted, "if Christ were here today, he would be branded a radical, a militant, and would probably be branded as 'red.'" Christ was a "revolutionary person, out there where it was happening. That's what God is all about, and that's where I get my strength." Summing up her life's work, she explained, "we can't separate Christ from freedom, and freedom from Christ." She criticized southern churches for doing "too much pretending and not enough actual working, the white ministers and the black ministers standing behind a podium and preaching a lie on Sunday." It was "long *past* time for the churches to wake up" and address fundamental issues of justice. Women such as Fannie Lou Hamer "placed Jesus where his experiences, as passed through the traditions of the Black church, could be used in the freedom struggle."[79]

Conclusion: The Ambiguity of the Southern Jesus in the Civil Rights Era

Once Jesus became an ally of the movement, he could no longer sanctify segregation. But black southerners faced their own difficulties with employing religion in the movement. Who was to say that the suffering servant Jesus, so long emblematic of the connection between African Americans and Christ, would become the symbol of choice for a civil rights struggle that demanded activism on behalf of changes in this world. For critics of "the black church," the spirituality of black churches seemed disconnected from social ends. Gospel music praised Jesus to the heavens but did little to bring Jesus to earth. Sermons that induced spiritual emotion but motivated little active organization now had to use all of the cultural resources at their disposal to advance explicitly political aims.

Anne Moody's story of *Coming of Age in Mississippi* suggests the kinds of inner turmoil many others felt. Her memoirs speak to generational conflicts in black communities between those comfortable with God as a white father and those who challenged the white establishment and the white God at the same time. Moody's skepticism later grew into a frontal assault against relying on Christian nonviolent civil disobedience to resolve racial problems. Before then, the white Christ of the white South seemed unable to survive the moral force of nonviolent resistance embodied in civil rights protests. Moody's ambivalence, her emotionally compelling participation in the movement and spiritual anger arising from countless other acts of violence, emerged from a long history of race and religion in America.

Anne Moody's baptism in her small Mississippi town at age eleven in 1951 was a big event. Parishioners dressed up in their Sunday best, and the initiates were decked out in baptismal white. Moody resented herself for caving in to the pressure exerted by her mother and churchwomen to be saved and baptized. Rather than venting her anger, she adopted the language of whiteness as purity: "I looked at that white dress, those white socks, that white slip, and those white drawers, and thought, 'This shit means I've been washed clean of all my sins!'" Later, in college, she threw herself into the civil rights movement. Like many of her generation, the movement became her church, her religion, and she deified its heroes: "I thought Bob Moses, the director of SNCC in Mississippi, was Jesus Christ in the flesh. A lot of other people thought of him as Jesus Christ, too." She participated in visits to white churches in Jackson, Mississippi, where ushers physically removed her and white churchgoers sometimes ostracized her. Finally she found some acceptance at an Episcopal Church. The seeming normality of the service could not contain its nerve-racking spiritual potency: "It was as normal as any church service. However, it was by no means normal to me. I was sitting there thinking any moment God would strike the life out of me. I recognized some of the whites, sitting around me in that church. If they were praying to the same God I was, then even God, I thought was against me."[80]

The freedom songs she joined in also confronted her with Jesus's ambiguity as a figure both consoling and challenging. Congregants at meetings sang freedom songs "as though they were singing away the chains of slavery." But the expressions on their faces gave her cold chills. Whenever God was mentioned, "I could tell by the way they said the word that most of them had given up here on earth. They seemed to be waiting just for God to call them home and end all the suffering." Listening to older Negroes sing, "I knew that it was the idea of heaven that kept them going. To them heaven would end their troubles. But listening to the teen-agers, I got an entirely different feeling. They felt that the power to change things was in themselves. More so than in God or anything else." Jesus as comforter and Jesus as nonviolent avenger inhabited the same church pews, inspiring while also separating older and younger parishioners.[81]

Moody knew about a merciful God but had seen that philosophy turned against black southerners. They had been the "humble, peace-loving, religious people," and yet they were the ones "doing all the suffering, as if they themselves were responsible for the killing and other acts committed against them." After the tragic bombing of the Sixteenth Street Baptist church in Birmingham in September 1963, Moody queried God about race and injustice: "Are you going to forgive their killers? You not gonna answer me, God, hmm?" For her, nonviolence had become too passive, for it caved in to whites' desire for the thrill of dominance through a violence directed against the sacred. "If you don't believe that," she wrote to God, "then I know you must be white, too. And if I ever find out that you are white, then I'm through with you. And if I find out you are black, I'll try my best to kill you when I get to heaven."[82]

Jesus had been born in both the white and black southern imaginations in the era of the Great Awakening. The Southern Jesus— the one who identified with the suffering—arose in the nineteenth century and had been given a white rebirth after the Civil War. Through the mid-twentieth century, artists, intellectuals, and activists reclaimed Jesus as an ally of movements for social justice. By the later 1960s, Jesus no longer could be such an unambiguously empathetic figure. Critics from the secular left, from inside the Student Nonviolent Coordinating Committee, and from the Black Muslims and the Black Panthers condemned the white Jesus of American history. While black southern Christians such as Fannie Lou Hamer never lost their faith in Christ's revolutionary nature, many others did. They perceived the unbearable whiteness of Christ in American history as too great to overcome.

All these varied responses to the figure of Jesus—from the Christ who literally suffered alongside the slaves to the suffering Lost Cause martyr, to the black Christs created by vernacular artists and theologians, to the civil rights Jesus exalted by figures such as Martin Luther King—sprang from the tumultuous history of a region riven by social conflicts. Ultimately, the Jesus of the South was a suffering saint readily adaptable to a variety of social conditions by both whites and blacks. The Jesus of the South, in all his complexity, arose from the long history of religion, race, and southern ideas of freedom. And his ambiguity as suffering saint left narrative holes that tricksters and Absalom stories filled in. Deeply embedded though he was in southern history and culture, Jesus only was not enough.

Notes

Chapter One. Moses, Jesus, Absalom, and the Trickster

1. Data originally compiled from the 2001 American Religious Identification Survey and posted at http://www.americanreligionsurvey-aris.org/reports /aris_2008_report_contents.html. This research originally was conducted as part of a larger eight-volume Religion by Region series, with the volume on the evangelical South published as Charles Reagan Wilson and Mark Silk, eds., *Religion and Public Life in the South: In the Evangelical Mode* (Walnut Creek, Calif.: AltaMira Press, 2005). This volume, in which I participated, excluded some states from the western and upland South (including Oklahoma, Arkansas, Kentucky, and others; inclusion of data from these states, grouped in this project as the "Southern Crossroads" region, would only accentuate the distinctiveness of the South as a whole in its evangelical orientation. Ted Ownby's piece in the *Religion and Public Life in the South* volume provides a great deal more of the statistical/demographic context discussed here. Research on these statistics also came from generous access provided to the data of the North American Religion Atlas project (http://www.religionatlas.org) compiled in 2000.

2. Data for this and the following paragraph are from the North American Religion Atlas.

3. Christine Heyrman, *Southern Cross: The Origins of the Bible Belt* (Chapel Hill: University of North Carolina Press, 1997). A survey of the literature on southern religion may be found in Randy J. Sparks, "Religion in the Pre–Civil War South," and Paul Harvey, "Religion in the American South since the Civil War," both in *A Companion to the American South*, ed. John Boles (Malden, Massachusetts: Blackwell Publishers, 2002), 156–75 and 387–406.

4. For murder rates, see the tables at http://www.deathpenaltyinfo.org /murder-rates-nationally-and-state. For gun violence per state, tables were compiled from http://bjsdata.ojp.usdoj.gov/dataonline/Search/Homicide /State/OneYearofData.cfm?NoVariables=Y&CFID=14377749&CFTO KEN=20439125. For infant mortality rates by state, see http://www.state healthfacts.org/comparemaptable.jsp?ind=47&cat=2. For obesity, where Mississippi, Louisiana, Kentucky, Oklahoma, West Virginia, and Tennessee lead the nation, see the obesity rates/maps provided by the Centers for Disease Control at http://www.cdc.gov/obesity/data/trends.html. For literacy rates, see the tables by state at http://nces.ed.gov/naal/estimates /StateEstimates.aspx.

5. Ulrich B. Phillips, "The Central Theme of Southern History," *American Historical Review* 34 (1928): 30–43; Wilbur J. Cash, *The Mind of the South* (New York: Knopf, 1941), 51.

6. C. J. Ryder, "The Theology of the Plantation Songs," *American Missionary*, January 1892, 15–16; Thomas Wentworth Higginson, "Negro Spirituals," *Atlantic Monthly*, June 1867, 685–94.

7. Lawrence Levine, *Black Culture and Black Consciousness: Afro-American Folk Thought from Slavery to Freedom* (New York: Oxford University Press, 1977), 50, 36.

8. Levine, *Black Culture and Black Consciousness*, 137; Norman Yetman, ed., *Life under the Peculiar Institution: Selections from the Slave Narrative Collection* (Huntington, N.Y.: R. E. Krieger, 1976), 164; Benjamin A. Botkin, ed., *Lay My Burden Down: A Folk History of Slavery* (Athens: University of Georgia Press, 1973), 16.

9. *American Missionary*, vol. 6 (February 1862), 33, as quoted in Albert Raboteau, *Slave Religion: The "Invisible Institution" in the Antebellum South* (New York: Oxford University Press, 1978), 320.

10. "Slavery and the Bible," *De Bow's Review* 9 (September 1850): 281–86, reprinted in Paul Finkelman, ed., *Defending Slavery: Proslavery Thought in the Old South, A Brief History with Documents* (Boston: Bedford Books, 2003); Elizabeth Fox-Genovese and Eugene D. Genovese, *The Mind of the Master Class: History and Faith in the Southern Slaveholders' Worldview* (Cambridge: Cambridge University Press, 2005), 510–11.

11. For more on how southern divines invoked both the Bible and their sense of History in defense of slaveholding as part of a godly social order that fought against the revolutionary tides of the era from the French Revolution forward, see Genovese and Genovese, *Mind of the Master Class*.

12. Kurt Berends, "'Wholesome Reading Purifies and Elevates the Man,': The Religious Military Press in the Confederacy," in *Religion and the American Civil War*, ed. Randall Miller et al. (New York: Oxford University Press, 1998), 148–49.

13. Daniel W. Stowell, "Stonewall Jackson and the Providence of God," in *Religion and the American Civil War*, 196; John Randolph Tucker, *The Southern Church Justified in the Support of the South in the Present War: A Lecture Delivered Before the Young Men's Christian Association of Richmond* (Richmond, Va.: W. H. Clemmitt, 1863), 33.

14. Charles Reagan Wilson, *Baptized in Blood: The Religion of the Lost Cause, 1865–1920* (Athens: University of Georgia Press, 1980), 71.

15. W. E. B. Du Bois, *The Negro Church*, ed. Phil Zuckerman et al. (1903; repr. Walnut Creek, Calif.: AltaMira Press, 2003), 36; Levine, *Black Culture and Black Consciousness*.

16. Aunt Katy's story from Christine Leigh Heyrman, *Southern Cross: The Beginnings of the Bible Belt* (Chapel Hill: University of North Carolina Press, 1997), 51, 198.

17. See Jason Young's analysis of the story in *Rituals of Resistance: African*

Atlantic Religion in Kongo and the Lowcountry South in the Era of Slavery (Baton Rouge: Louisiana State University Press, 2007).

18. Allan Callahan, *The Talking Book: African Americans and the Bible* (New Haven: Yale University Press, 2006), 187; Clifton Johnson, *God Struck Me Dead: Religious Conversion Experiences and Autobiographies of Ex-Slaves* (Philadelphia: Pilgrim Press, 1969), 60.

19. Levine, *Black Culture and Black Consciousness*, 36–37.

20. Ibid.; Mechal Sobel, *Trabelin' On: The Slave Journey to an Afro-Baptist Faith* (1978; repr. Princeton: Princeton University Press, 1988), 114.

21. Ibid., 118; a survey of lyrics from http://www.negrospirituals.com shows the prevalence of Jesus and Christ imagery in these songs.

22. The discussion of the rise of mass-produced images of the white Jesus comes from Edward J. Blum and Paul Harvey, *Jesus in Red, White, and Black: The Son of God and the Saga of Race in American History* (Chapel Hill: University of North Carolina Press, 2012).

23. Dwight Hopkins, "Slave Theology in the 'Invisible Institution,'" reprinted in *African American Religious Thought: An Anthology* (Louisville, Ky.: Westminster John Knox Press, 2003), 813; Callahan, *Talking Book*, 236.

24. Hopkins, "Slave Theology," 806.

25. Levine, *Black Culture and Black Consciousness*, 37, 43.

26. Ibid., 120.

27. Morgan Godwyn, *The Negro's and Indians Advocate, Suing for Their Admission Into the Church, or A Persuasive to the Instructing and Baptizing of the Negro's and Indians in Our Plantations* (London, 1680), 33; Michael A. Gomez, *Exchanging Our Country Marks: The Transformation of African Identities in the Colonial and Antebellum South* (Chapel Hill: University of North Carolina Press, 1998), 268, 283; Orra Langhorne, "Correspondence," *Southern Workman* 7 (September 1878): 67, reprinted in *Strange Ways and Sweet Dreams: Afro-American Folklore from the Hampton Institute*, ed. Donald Waters (Boston: G. K. Hall & Co., 1983), 145–47; Carl Carmer, *Stars Fell on Alabama* (New York: Farrar and Rinehart, 1934), 218; Yvonne Chireau, *Black Magic: Religion and the African American Conjuring Tradition* (Berkeley: University of California Press, 2003), 146.

28. Hortense Powdermaker, *After Freedom: A Cultural Study in the Deep South* (New York: Viking, 1939), 286.

29. See Chireau, *Black Magic*, and Jeffrey Anderson, *Conjure in African American Society* (Baton Rouge: Louisiana State University Press, 2005).

30. See Blind Lemon Jefferson, "Low Down Mojo Blues," track 12, disc 3 of *Classic Sides* (JSP Records, 2003); James Cone, *The Spirituals and the Blues* (1972; repr. New York: Orbis Books, 1992); Jon Michael Spencer, *Blues and Evil* (Knoxville: University of Tennessee Press, 1993), 64–66.

31. Cone, *The Spirituals and the Blues*, 108; Spencer, *Blues and Evil*, 11; Charley Patton, "High Water Rising," tracks 3 and 4 on CD 2 of Charley Patton, *Complete Recordings, 1929–1934* (JSP Records, 2002).

32. William Wells Brown, *My Southern Home* (Boston: A. G. Brown,

1880), 21–22, 68; Chireau, *Black Magic*, 19; Waters, *Strange Ways and Sweet Dreams*, 146.

33. Gillian Welch, "Caleb Meyer," track 1 on CD *Hell among the Yearlings* (Acony Records, 1998).

34. Blum develops the idea of the trickster Jesus in our coauthored book, *Jesus in Red, White, and Black: The Son of God and the Saga of Race in American History* (Chapel Hill: University of North Carolina Press, 2012).

35. William Faulkner, *Absalom, Absalom!* (New York: Vintage International Edition, 1990), 14. All page references are to this edition.

36. Thadious Davis, "The Signifying Abstraction: Reading 'the Negro' in *Absalom, Absalom!*," reprinted in *Absalom, Absalom!: A Casebook*, ed. Fred Hobson (New York: Oxford University Press, 2003), 81.

37. C. Vann Woodward, "The Search for Southern Identity," in *The Burden of Southern History*, enlarged ed. (Baton Rouge: Louisiana State University Press, 1977), 21.

38. Eric Sundquist, "*Absalom, Absalom!* and the House Divided," reprinted in *William Faulkner's Absalom, Absalom!: A Case Book*, 144.

39. See Mark Reinhardt, *Who Speaks for Margaret Garner?* (Minneapolis: University of Minnesota Press, 2010).

40. Toni Morrison, *Beloved* (New York: Vintage International, 2004). All page references are to this edition.

41. Edward P. Jones, *The Known World* (New York: Harper Paperbacks, 2004), 8–9. All page references are to this edition.

Chapter Two. "'Because I Was a Master'"

1. Charles Colcock Jones, *The Religious Instruction of the Negroes: A Sermon, Delivered Before Associations of Planters in Liberty and McIntosh Counties Georgia, by the Rev. Charles Colcock Jones of Savannah* (Princeton: D'Hart & Connolly, 1832), 26; Erskine Clarke, *Dwelling Place: A Plantation Epic* (New Haven, Conn.: Yale University Press, 2005).

2. Charles Colcock Jones, *Tenth Annual Report of the Liberty County Association for the Instruction of the Negroes in Liberty County, Georgia* (Savannah, Ga., 1845), 24–25; also quoted in Albert Raboteau, *Slave Religion: The "Invisible Institution" in the Antebellum South* (New York: Oxford University Press, 1978), 294. Also see Charles Colcock Jones, *The Religious Instruction of the Negroes in the United States* (Savannah, Ga.: Thomas Purse, 1842), available at "Documenting the American South," http://docsouth.unc.edu/church/jones/menu.html.

3. Chris Beneke, *Beyond Toleration: The Religious Origins of American Pluralism* (New York: Oxford University Press, 2006); Chris Beneke and Christopher S. Grenda, *The First Prejudice: Religious Tolerance and Intolerance in Early America* (Philadelphia: University of Pennsylvania Press, 2011); David Sehat, *The Myth of American Religious Freedom* (New York: Oxford University Press, 2010).

4. Nathan Hatch, *The Democratization of American Christianity* (New Haven, Conn.: Yale University Press, 1989); Mark Noll, *America's God: From Jonathan Edwards to Abraham Lincoln* (New York: Oxford University Press, 2002).

5. Reprinted at "The Practise of Slavery" section of the Virtual Jamestown Project, at http://www.virtualjamestown.org/practise.html, and also quoted in Raboteau, *Slave Religion*, 100; Michael Gomez, *Exchanging Our Country Marks: The Transformation of African Identities in the Colonial and Antebellum South* (Chapel Hill: University of North Carolina Press, 1998), 247. Final quote from Winthrop Jordan, *White Over Black: American Attitudes Toward the Negro, 1550–1812* (Chapel Hill: University of North Carolina Press, 1968), 24.

6. Morgan Godwyn, *The Negro's and Indians Advocate, Suing for Their Admission to the Church* (London, 1680), 33; Raboteau, *Slave Religion*, 65; Jordan, *White Over Black*, 20.

7. Rebecca Anne Goetz, "From Potential Christians to Hereditary Heathens: Religion and Race in the Early Chesapeake, 1590–1740" (PhD diss., Harvard University, 2006).

8. The Maryland and Virginia laws are reprinted in a number of places, including Kai Wright, ed., *The African American Experience: Black History and Culture through Speeches, Letters, Editorials, Poems, Songs, and Stories* (New York: Black Dog & Leventhal Publishers, 2009), 27; June Purcell Guild, *Black Laws of Virginia: A Summary of the Legislative Acts of Virginia Concerning Negroes from the Earliest Times to the Present* (1936; repr. New York: Negro Universities Press and Greenwood Publishing Group, 1969). A readily accessible full compilation of these laws is available online at http://www.virtualjamestown.org/slavelink.html.

9. Goetz, "Potential Christians to Hereditary Heathens," 211; Hugh Jones, *The Present State of Virginia* (1724; repr. New York, 1865), 71. This classic and indispensable primary source is readily available online at Project Gutenberg: http://www.gutenberg.org/ebooks/29055.

10. Goetz, "Potential Christians to Hereditary Heathens," 142–45. Original law from William Waller Hening, ed., *The Statutes at Large: Being a Collection of All the Laws of Virginia* (New York: R. W. G. & Barlow, 1819–1823), 2:260. For most students, the single most convenient and accessible way to survey colonial Virginia's laws regarding slavery, including the 1667 and 1705 provisions quoted above, is now available through the Virtual Jamestown project, at http://www.virtualjamestown.org/slavelink.html.

11. Frank Klingberg, ed., *An Appraisal of the Negro in South Carolina: A Study in Americanization* (Washington, D.C.: Associated Publishers, 1941), 29.

12. Peter Kalm, *Travels into North America*, reprinted in *A General Collection of the Best and Most Interesting Voyages and Travels in All parts of the World*, ed. John Pinkerton (London, 1812), 503.

13. Thomas Ingersoll, "'Releese us out of this Cruell Bondegg': An Appeal from Virginia in 1723," *William and Mary Quarterly*, 3rd ser., 54 (October 1994): 777–82.

14. Francis Le Jau to the Secretary, 15 September 1708, in *The Carolina Chronicle of Dr. Francis Le Jau, 1706–1717*, ed. Frank J. Klingberg (Berkeley: University of California Press, 1956), 41. Future references will omit "Le Jau to the Secretary" and other salutations and just list the date of the letter and page number.

15. Sylvia Frey and Betty Wood, *Come Shouting to Zion: African American Protestantism in the American South and British Caribbean to 1830* (Chapel Hill: University of North Carolina Press, 1998), 65; Klingberg, ed., *Carolina Chronicle*, 22 March, 1708/09, 55; 5 August 1709, 58; 13 June 1710, 79.

16. Raboteau, *Slave Religion*, 123.

17. Klingberg, ed., *Negro in Colonial South Carolina*, 6–7.

18. Klingberg, ed., *Carolina Chronicle*, 18 September 1711, 102; 11 December 1712, 125; 23 February 1712/1713, 130.

19. Klingberg, ed., *Carolina Chronicle*, 1 February 1709/10, 70.

20. Klingberg, ed., *Negro in Colonial South Carolina*, 47, 56.

21. Ira Berlin, *Generations of Captivity: A History of African American Slaves* (Cambridge, Mass.: Harvard University Press, 2003), 44.

22. Stono rebellion document from http://www.pbs.org/wgbh/aia/part1/1h311t.html; John Thornton, "African Dimensions of the Stono Rebellion," *American Historical Review* 96, no. 4 (October 1991): 1103; Mark Smith, "Remembering Mary, Shaping Revolt: Understanding the Stono Rebellion," *Journal of Southern History* 67 (August 2001): 513–34.

23. Frey and Wood, *Come Shouting to Zion*, 93–94.

24. Davies material in previous two paragraphs from Frey and Wood, *Come Shouting to Zion*, 98; Samuel Davies, "On Virginia's Christian Slaves," quoted in Thomas Kidd, ed., *The Great Awakening: A Brief History with Documents*, (Boston: Bedford Books, 2008), 118–19; Samuel Davies, *Letters from the Rev. Samuel Davies, &c. Shewing the state of religion (particularly among the Negroes) in Virginia* (London, 1757), 28–31; Goetz, "Potential Christian to Hereditary Heathens," 263.

25. Samuel Davies, *Letters*, 29–30; Frey and Wood, *Come Shouting to Zion*, 110–11.

26. Michael Gomez, *Exchanging Our Country Marks*, 254.

27. Raboteau, *Slave Religion*, 146–47.

28. John Marrant, *Narrative of John Marrant*, quoted in Kidd, ed., *The Great Awakening*, 86–88. The full narrative is also available at http://www.blackloyalist.com/canadiandigitalcollection/documents/diaries/marrant_narrative.htm.

29. Jeffrey Robert Young, *Domesticating Slavery: The Master Class in South Carolina and Georgia, 1670–1837* (Chapel Hill: University of North Carolina Press, 1999), 143.

30. Jones, *Religious Instruction of the Negroes in the United States*, 195, 201, 159–60.

31. Winthrop Jordan, *The White Man's Burden: Historical Origins of Racism in the United States* (New York: Oxford University Press, 1974), 10.

32. John Fletcher, *Studies on Slavery, in Easy Lessons* (Natchez: J. Warner, 1852), 453–77, see especially 473. A succinct summary may be found in H. Shelton Smith, *In His Image but . . . : Racism in Southern Religion, 1780–1910* (Durham, N.C.: Duke University Press, 1972), 131.

33. Eugene Genovese and Elizabeth Fox-Genovese, *Mind of the Master Class: History and Faith in the Southern Slaveholders' Worldview* (Cambridge: Cambridge University Press, 2004), 526.

34. Mark Noll, *The Civil War as a Theological Crisis* (Princeton, N.J.: Princeton University Press, 2006), 56, 74.

35. See Paul Harvey, "The Christian Doctrine of Slavery," in *Religions of the United States in Practice*, ed. Colleen McDannell, vol. 1 (Princeton, N.J.: Princeton University Press, 2002).

36. "Slavery and the Bible," *DeBow's Review* (September 1850), 281–86, reprinted in *Defending Slavery: Proslavery Thought in the Old South: A Brief History with Documents*, ed. Paul Finkelman (Boston: Bedford Books, 2003), 113–14; Thornton Stringfellow, "The Bible Argument, or, Slavery in the Light of Divine Revelation," in Finkelman, ed., *Defending Slavery*, 128.

37. James Henley Thornwell, "The Christian Doctrine of Slavery," in *The Collected Writings of James Henley Thornwell*, ed. John B. Adger and John L. Girardeau, vol. 4, *Ecclesiastical* (Richmond: Presbyterian Committee on Publication, 1873), 399.

38. Ibid., 403, 414.

39. Ibid., 410.

40. David Chesebrough, ed., *"God Ordained This War": Sermons on the Sectional Crisis, 1830–1865* (Columbia: University of South Carolina Press), 204–5.

41. Gomez, *Exchanging Our Country Marks*, 259.

42. Minerva Grubbs interview in George Rawick, ed., *The American Slave: A Composite Autobiography* (Westport, Conn.: Greenwood Press, 1972–1979), series 1, *Mississippi*, vol. 8, part 3, pp. 892–93. Also see Gomez, *Exchanging Our Country Marks*, 268–69, and Shane White and Graham White, *The Sounds of Slavery: Discovering African American History through Songs, Sermon, and Speech* (Boston: Beacon Press, 2005), 106.

43. Anderson Edwards, "Two Ways of Preaching the Gospel," in *Lay My Burden Down: A Folk History of Slavery*, ed. B. A. Botkin (1945; Athens: University of Georgia Press, 1989), 26.

44. Kenneth Greenberg, ed., *The Confessions of Nat Turner and Related Documents* (Boston: Bedford Books, 1996), 45–47.

45. *Constitutional Whig*, August 29, 1831, reprinted in Greenberg, ed., *Confessions of Nat Turner*, 64–66; *Richmond Enquirer*, August 30, 1831, reprinted in Greenberg, *Confessions of Nat Turner*, 67–68.

46. *Constitutional Whig*, September 26, 1831, reprinted in Greenberg, ed., *Confessions of Nat Turner*, 80.

47. Letter from Virginia governor John Floyd to South Carolina governor

James Hamilton, November 19, 1831, reprinted in Greenberg, ed., *Confessions of Nat Turner*, 109–12.

48. Thomas Wentworth Higginson, "Negro Spirituals," *Atlantic Monthly*, June 1867, available also at http://xroads.virginia.edu/~hyper/twh/higg.html.

49. Frederick Douglass, *Narrative of the Life of Frederick Douglass, An American Slave* (Boston, 1845), 119; Frederick Douglass, "The Southern Style of Preaching to Slaves," address delivered January 1, 1842, in *The Frederick Douglass Papers: Speeches, Debates, and Interviews*, ed. John W. Blassingame and John R. McKivigan, vol. 1, *1841–46* (New Haven, Conn.: Yale University Press, 2001), 17.

50. Frederick Douglass, "American Slavery, American Religion, and the Free Church of Scotland: An Address Delivered in London, England, on May 22, 1846," reprinted in Frederick Douglass, *My Bondage and My Freedom*, ed. John Stauffer (New York: Modern Library, 2003), 252. Also available at the Gilder Lehrman Center for the Study of Slavery, Resistance, and Abolition, at http://www.yale.edu/glc/archive/1077.htm.

51. This theme of the "subversive savior" and the "trickster of the Trinity" comes from Edward J. Blum, who develops the concepts in our coauthored book, *Jesus in Red, White, and Black: The Son of God and the Saga of Race in American History* (Chapel Hill: University of North Carolina Press, forthcoming 2012).

Chapter Three. Suffering Saint

1. *The Apostle*, directed by Robert Duvall, 1997.
2. Wilbur J. Cash, *Mind of the South* (New York: Knopf, 1941), 58.
3. Faulkner reference from Charles Reagan Wilson, "William Faulkner and the Southern Religious Culture," chapter 4 in *Judgment and Grace in Dixie*, 2nd ed. (Athens, Georgia: University of Georgia Press, 2007), 55.
4. Lillian Smith, *Killers of the Dream* (1949; repr. New York: Norton, 1994), 103; Cash, *Mind of the South*, 58.
5. David Burgess, "Preachers, Beware!" *Prophetic Religion* 6 (Summer 1945): 37–38; Myles Horton, *The Long Haul*, 2nd ed (New York: Teachers College Press, 1998), 26, 29; Richard Callahan, *Work and Faith in the Kentucky Coal Fields: Subject to Dust* (Bloomington: Indiana University Press, 2008), 13, 197; Jarod Roll, *Spirit of Rebellion: Labor and Religion in the New Cotton South* (Urbana: University of Illinois Press, 2009).
6. Du Bois quotation from "The Church and the Negro," *Crisis*, December 1913, 290–91.
7. Erskine Clarke, *Dwelling Place: A Plantation Epic* (New Haven: Yale University Press, 2005); Charles Colcock Jones, "The Religious Instructions of the Negroes," in *God Ordained This War: Sermons on the Sectional Crisis, 1830–1865* (Columbia: University of South Carolina Press, 1991), 171; William Meade, *Pastoral Letter of the Right Rev. William Meade, Assistant Bishop of Virginia, to the Ministers, Members, and Friends, of the Protestant

Episcopal Church in the Diocese of Virginia, of the Duty of Affording Religious Instruction to Those in Bondage (Richmond, Va.: H. K. Ellyson, 1853), 8–12.

8. Michael Pasquier, "'Though Their Skin Remains Brown, I Hope Their Souls Will Soon be White': Slavery, French Missionaries, and the Roman Catholic Priesthood in the American South, 1789–1865," *Church History* 77, no. 2 (June 2008): 337, 356.

9. Henry Brown, *Narrative of Henry Box Brown, Who Escaped from Slavery Enclosed in a Box 3 Feet Long and 2 Wide. Written from a Statement of Facts Made by Himself. With Remarks Upon The Remedy for Slavery* (Boston: Charles Stearns, 1849), 16–17.

10. Material from George Rawick, ed., *The American Slave: A Composite Autobiography* (Westport, Conn.: Greenwood Press, 1972–1979). Quotations taken from the following specific volumes: "R. L. D., *Alabama Narratives*, vol. 1, 175; George Briggs, *South Carolina Narratives*, vol. 14, part 1, 7; Estella Jones, *Georgia Narratives*, vol. 4, part 2, 345; Cordelia Jackson, *South Carolina Narratives*, vol. 14, part 3, 5.

11. James Watkins, *Narrative of the Life of James Watkins; Formerly a "Chattel" in Maryland, U.S.; Containing an Account of His Escape from Slavery, Together with an Appeal on Behalf of Three Millions of Such "Pieces of Property," Still Held Under the Standard of the Eagle* (Bolton: Kenyon and Abbatt, 1852), 16–17; Martha Griffith Browne, *Autobiography of a Female Slave* (New York: Redfield, 1857); Noah Davis, *A Narrative of the Life of Rev. Noah David, A Colored Man, Written by Himself, at the Age of Fifty-Four* (Baltimore: John F. Weishampel, 1859), 24. All texts available from "Documenting the American South," at http://docsouth.unc.edu.

12. Peter Randolph, *Sketches of Slave Life: Or, Illustrations of the Peculiar Institution* (Published for author, 1855), 25–26, 34.

13. Octavia V. Rogers Albert, *THE HOUSE OF BONDAGE: OR, Charlotte Brooks and other Slaves, Original and Life Like, As They Appeared in Their Old Plantation and City Slave Life; Together with Pen-Pictures of the Peculiar Institution, With Sights and Insights Into Their New Relations as Freedmen, Freeman, and Citizens* (New York: Hunt & Eaton, 1890), pp. 32–34. Available from "Documenting the American South," at http://docsouth.unc.edu.

14. Allan Callahan, *The Talking Book: African Americans and the Bible* (New Haven: Yale University Press, 2006), 201.

15. Charlotte Forten, "Life on the Sea Islands," *Atlantic Monthly*, May 1864, 253.

16. Henry L. Swint, ed., *Dear Ones at Home: Letters from Contraband Camps* (Nashville: Vanderbilt University Press, 1966), 91. Also quoted in Charles Irons, *The Origins of Proslavery Christianity: White and Black Evangelicals in Colonial and Antebellum Virginia* (Chapel Hill: University of North Carolina Press, 2007), 253.

17. Thomas Wentworth Higginson, *Army Life in a Black Regiment*, ed. by Howard N. Meyer (1870; repr., New York: Norton, 1984), 192, 202, 209.

18. "The American War versus the European War," *Douglass' Monthly*, July 1859.

19. Ella Gertrude Clanton Thomas, *The Secret Eye: The Journal of Ella Gertrude Clanton Thomas*, ed. Virginia Burr (Chapel Hill: University of North Carolina Press, 1990), 276.

20. Irons, *The Origins of Proslavery Christianity*, 260; Daniel Stowell, *Rebuilding Zion: The Religious Reconstruction of the South, 1863–1877* (New York: Oxford, 1998), 36.

21. Wilson, *Baptized in Blood*, 75; J. W. Tucker, "God's Providence in War," in *"God Ordained This War": Sermons on the Sectional Crisis, 1830–1865*, ed. David B. Chesebrough (Columbia: University of South Carolina Press, 1991), 236.

22. Lloyd Hunter, "The Immortal Confederacy: Another Look at Lost Cause Religion," in *The Myth of the Lost Cause and Civil War Memory*, eds. Gary Gallagher and Alan T. Nolan (Bloomington: Indiana University Press, 2000), 185–216.

23. Hunter, "The Immortal Confederacy," 204.

24. John William Jones, *Christ in the Camp; or, Religion in Lee's Army* (Richmond, Va.: B. F. Johnson & Co., 1887), 326, 344, 373, 430, 206–7.

25. Gardiner H. Shattuck Jr., *A Shield and a Hiding Place: The Religious Life of the Civil War Armies* (Macon, Ga.: Mercer University Press, 1985), 123–24; Hunter, "The Immortal Confederacy," 190–97. For more on this kind of sanctification of Lee, see Wilson, *Baptized in Blood*, 45–49, 128–129.

26. Hunter, "The Immortal Confederacy," 200, 208.

27. Jones, *Christ in the Camp*, 20; Amy Louise Wood, *Lynching and Spectacle: Witnessing Racial Violence in America, 1890–1940* (Chapel Hill: University of North Carolina Press, 2009), 45–47.

28. Laura J. Veltman, "(Re)producing White Supremacy: Race, the Protestant Church, and the American Family in the Works of Thomas Dixon, Jr.," in *Vale of Tears: New Essays on Religion and Reconstruction*, eds. Edward J. Blum and W. Scott Poole (Macon, Ga.: Mercer University Press, 2005), 248–54.

29. Robert Watson Sledge, "A History of the Methodist Episcopal Church South, 1914–1939" (PhD diss., University of Texas, Austin, 1972), 186–88; Glenn Feldman, *Politics, Society, and the Klan in Alabama, 1915–1949* (Tuscaloosa: University of Alabama Press, 1999), 37–40, 59.

30. Quotations from Kelly J. Baker, "The Gospel According to the Klan: The Ku Klux Klan's Vision of White Protestant America, 1915–1930" (PhD diss., Florida State University, 2007), 40–46. Now published as Kelly J. Baker, *Gospel According to the Klan: The KKK's Appeal to Protestant America, 1915–1930* (Lawrence: University Press of Kansas, 2011).

31. Henry McNeal Turner, *Respect Black: The Writings and Speeches of Henry McNeal Turner*, ed. Edwin Redkey (New York: Arno Press, 1971), 176, originally published in *Voice of Missions*, April 5, 1898.

32. Henry McNeal Turner, "The Negro and the Fatherland," in *Africa and*

the American Negro: Addresses and Proceedings of the Congress on Africa, Held Under the Auspices of the Steward Missionary Foundation for Africa of Gammon Theological Seminary, In Connection with the Cotton States and International Exposition, December 13–15, 1895, ed. J. W. E. Bowen (Atlanta: Gammon Theological Seminary, 1896), 197.

33. James Morris Webb, *The Black Man: The Father of Civilization Proven by Biblical History* (1918), and Webb, *A Black Man Will be The Coming Universal King Proven by Biblical History* (1918). Webb's sermon and further information about his life and work can be found on Rev. Webb, "Moses Was Rescued by a Negro Woman," on the six-CD set *Goodbye Babylon* (Atlanta: Dust-to-Digital, 2003), disc 6, track 15.

34. W. L. Hunter, *Jesus Christ Had Negro Blood in His Veins: The Wonder of the 20th Century* (self-published, orig. edition 1901), 20.

35. John Giggie, "God's Long Journey: African Americans, Religion, and History in the Mississippi Delta, 1875–1915" (PhD diss., Princeton University, 1997), 201; Randy Sparks, *Religion in Mississippi* (Jackson: University Press of Mississippi, 2001), 173; Jones in Dupree Collection, box 1, folder 12, Schomburg Center for Research in Black Culture, New York, Public Library; Charles P. Jones to Isaac Bailey, March 26, 1898, in Bailey-Thurman Papers, Emory Special Collections Library, Emory University, Atlanta, Georgia.

36. Jon Michael Spencer, *Black Hymnody: A Hymnological History of the African-American Church* (Knoxville: University of Tennessee Press, 1992), 103–5, 114–15.

37. Giggie, "God's Long Journey," 213; Mary Mason, ed., *The History and Life Work of Bishop C. H. Mason*, orig. 1924, recompiled 1987, 88, 92, 94, copy in Dupree Collection, Schomburg Center for Research in Black Culture; David Tucker, *Black Pastors and Leaders: Memphis, 1819–1972* (Memphis: Memphis State University Press, 1975), 87–100.

38. Callahan, *Talking Book*, 232.

39. Letter from James Wentworth Leigh, Butler's Island, Darien, Georiga,1874, reprinted in *Ten Years on a Georgia Plantation since the War* (1883; repr. New York: Negro Universities Press, 1969), 374.

40. Skip James, "Jesus Is a Mighty Good Leader," recorded 1930–31, on CD recording *The Complete Early Recordings of Skip James* (Yazoo Records, 1994), track 7.

41. Selections from *American Primitive, Vol. I: Raw Pre-War Gospel* (CD, Revenant Records, 1997), tracks 8 and 23.

42. Lawrence Levine, *Black Culture and Black Consciousness: Afro-American Folk Thought from Slavery to Freedom* (New York: Oxford University Press, 1977), 175. Recordings of both songs and informative liner notes about the history of Dorsey's early works may be found in the six-CD set *Goodbye Babylon* (Dust-to-Digital Music, Atlanta, Georgia, 2003).

43. Washington Phillips, "Denomination Blues, Part I and Part II," on CD recording *I Am Born to Preach the Gospel* (Yazoo Records, 1991), tracks 7 and 8; John Giggie, *After Redemption: Jim Crow and the Transformation of African*

American Religion in the Delta, 1875–1915 (New York: Oxford University Press, 2008), 3–4, 45, 57.

44. Paul Oliver, *Songsters and Saints: Vocal Traditions on Race Records* (Cambridge: Cambridge University Press, 1984), 180, 199; Evelyn Brooks Higginbotham, "Rethinking Vernacular Culture: Black Religion and Race Records in the 1920s and 1930s," in *African American Religious Thought: An Anthology*, eds. Cornel West and Eddie Glaude Jr. (Lexington, Ky.: Westminster John Knox Press, 2003), 986.

45. Giggie, *After Redemption*, 155.

46. See John Hayes, "Hard, Hard Religion: Faith and Class in the New South" (PhD diss., University of Georgia, 2007).

47. Hayes, "Hard, Hard Religion," 305, 196.

48. Zora Neale Hurston, *Dust Tracks on a Road* (1942; repr. New York: Harper Perennial, 1996), 275, 280; Zora Neale Hurston, *The Sanctified Church* (Berkeley, Calif.: Turtle Island Press, 1983), 83.

49. Hurston, *The Sanctified Church*, 88–89; Carter Woodson, *The Rural Negro* (Washington, D.C.: Association for the Study of Negro Life and History, 1930), 163–64.

50. Callahan, *Talking Book*, 39, 216–17; August Wilson, *Joe Turner's Come and Gone* (script from Samuel French, Inc., 1986), 132; Alice Walker, *The Color Purple* (New York: Washington Square Press, 1982), 194.

51. Quoted from Charles Reagan Wilson, "'Just a Little Talk with Jesus': Elvis Presley, Religious Music, and Southern Spirituality," *Southern Cultures* 12 (2006): 74–91.

52. George Vecsey, "Cash's 'Gospel Road' Film is Renaissance for Him," orig. 1973, repr. in *Ring of Fire: The Johnny Cash Reader*, ed. Michael Streissguth (Cambridge, Mass.: Da Capo Press, 2002), 126.

53. Ted Olsen, "Johnny Cash's Song of Redemption," *Christianity Today* 47 (November 2003), reprinted in *Ring of Fire: The Johnny Cash Reader*, ed. Michael Streissguth (Cambridge, Mass.: Da Capo Press, 2002), 60–62.

54. "The Beast in Me" and "Redemption" from *American Recordings* (CD, Lost Highway Records, 1994), tracks 4 and 11; Billy Jo Shaver, "Jesus Was Our Savior, Cotton Was Our King," on CD recording *Old Five and Dimers Like Me* (Koch Records, 1996), track 8; CD; "Personal Jesus" from Johnny Cash, *American IV: The Man Comes Around* (CD, Lost Highway, 2002), track 7. >

55. Benjamin Mays, *The Negro's God, as Reflected in His Literature* (Boston: Chapman & Grimes, 1938); E. Franklin Frazier, *Negro Youth at the Crossways: Their Personality Development in the Middle States* (Washington, D.C.: American Council on Education, 1940).

56. Howard Thurman, *Jesus and the Disinherited* (1949; repr. Boston: Beacon Press, 1996), 43.

57. Jennifer L. Strychasz, "'Jesus is Black': Race and Christianity in African-American Church Art, 1968–1986" (PhD diss., University of Maryland, 2003), 58.

58. Strychasz, "Jesus Is Black," 32, 55.

59. Richard J. Powell, "'In My Family of Primitiveness and Tradition': William H. Johnson's *Jesus and the Three Marys*," *American Art* 5 (Autumn 1991): 21–33.

60. Carol Crown, ed., *Coming Home: Self-Taught Artists, the Bible, and the American South* (Memphis: Art Museum of the University of Memphis, 2002); Cheryl Rivers, "Clementine Hunter: Chronicler of African American Catholicism," in *Sacred and Profane: Voice and Vision in Southern Self-Taught Art*, ed. Carol Crown and Charles Russell (Jackson: University Press of Mississippi, 2007), 146–72.

61. Information on Anderson Johnson from http://web.wm.edu/middle passage/exhibits/johnson/?svr=wwwURL, and from Crown, *Coming Home*.

62. William Fagaly, *Sister Gertrude Morgan: The Tools of Her Ministry* (New York: Rizzoli, 2004). A portion of this work is conveniently excerpted for an accompanying exhibition at the New Orleans Museum of Art, available at http://www.noma.org/educationguides/Morgan.pdf.

63. John Henrik Clarke, "The Boy Who Painted Christ Black," in *Brothers and Sisters*, ed. Arnold Adoff (New York: Dell, 1970), 55–62.

64. Howell Raines, ed., *My Soul Is Rested: Movement Days in the Deep South Remembered* (New York: Penguin, 1983), 53; David Chappell, *A Stone of Hope: Prophetic Religion and the Death of Jim Crow* (Chapel Hill: University of North Carolina Press, 2004), 56; Clayborne Carson, "Martin Luther King, Jr., and the African American Social Gospel," in Cornel West and Eddie Glaude, eds., *African American Religious Thought*, 701.

65. Martin Luther King Jr., *Stride Toward Freedom: The Montgomery Story* (New York: Harper, 1958), 134–35; King, *Strength to Love* (New York: Harper & Row, 1963), 106–7; David Garrow, "Martin Luther King, Jr., and the Spirit of Leadership," *Journal of American History* 74 (September 1987): 442; Lewis V. Baldwin, *There is a Balm in Gilead: The Cultural Roots of Martin Luther King, Jr* (Minneapolis: Fortress Press, 1991), 187–89; Stewart Burns, ed., *Daybreak of Freedom: The Montgomery Bus Boycott* (Chapel Hill: University of North Carolina Press, 1997), 17.

66. "Loving Your Enemies," sermon delivered at Dexter Avenue Baptist Church, November 17, 1957, in *The Papers of Martin Luther King, Jr.*, ed. Clayborne Carson et al., vol. 4, *Symbol of the Movement* (Berkeley: University of California Press, 2000), 323–24; Benjamin Mays interview in Howell Raines, ed., *My Soul is Rested: Movement Days in the Deep South Remembered* (1977; New York: Penguin, 1983), 449. Henceforth *The Papers of Martin Luther King, Jr.* will be cited simply as *King Papers*. For more on Mays, see Randal Maurice Jelks, *Schoolmaster of the Movement: Benjamin Elijah Mays, a Religious Rebel in Jim Crow America* (Chapel Hill: University of North Carolina Press, 2012).

67. "A Talk with Martin Luther King," December 1960, Cornell University, in *King Papers*, vol. 5, *Threshold of a New Decade*, 569.

68. Palm Sunday sermon on Mohandas K. Gandhi, delivered at Dexter Avenue Baptist Church, March 22, 1959, in *King Papers*, vol. 5, 146.

69. Martin Luther King, "My Pilgrimage to Nonviolence," September 1, 1958, in *King Papers*, vol. 5, 473-81; Martin Luther King, "An Experiment in Love," from *A Testament of Hope: The Essential Writings and Speeches of Martin Luther King, Jr.*, ed. James Melvin Washington Jr. (San Francisco: HarperCollins, 1986), 16.

70. From Clayborne Carson et al., eds., *The Eyes on the Prize Civil Rights Reader: Documents, Speeches, and Firsthand Accounts from the Black Freedom Struggle* (New York: Penguin, 1991), 49-50; "The Violence of Desperate Men," excerpt from *Stride Toward Freedom*, in *The Eyes on the Prize Civil Rights Reader*, p. 57.

71. "Christ Our Starting Point," sermon at Dexter Avenue Baptist Church, December 21, 1958, in *King Papers*, vol. 6, *Advocate of the Social Gospel*, September 1948–March 1963, 352-53.

72. Garrow, "Martin Luther King," 444; "Suffering and Faith," April 27, 1960, draft of material to be added into *Christian Century* article, in *King Papers*, vol. 5, 443-44.

73. Mrs. Pinkie Franklin to Martin Luther King Jr., January 31, 1956, in *Daybreak of Freedom: The Montgomery Bus Boycott*, ed. Stewart Burns (Chapel Hill: University of North Carolina Press, 1997), 136; Lewis interview in *My Soul is Rested*, 83.

74. Criswell quote from Paul Harvey, *Freedom's Coming: Religious Cultures and the Shaping of the South from the Civil War through the Civil Rights Era* (Chapel Hill: University of North Carolina Press, 2005), 244; Jane Dailey, "Sex, Segregation, and the Sacred: From Brown to Selma," *Journal of American History* 91 (2004): 119-44.

75. Charles Marsh, *God's Long Summer: Stories of Faith and Civil Rights* (Princeton: Princeton University Press, 1997), 55, 60-61, 82-90; Sparks, *Religion in Mississippi*, 228-31.

76. Taylor Branch, *Parting the Waters: America in the King Years, 1954–1963* (New York: Simon and Schuster, 1988), 339-40; Martin Luther King eulogy, September 18, 1963, reprinted at http://www.english.illinois.edu/Maps/poets/m_r/randall/birmingham.htm).

77. King, address to the First Annual Institute in Non-Violence and Social Change, December 1956, in *A Testament of Hope: The Essential Speeches and Writings of Martin Luther King, Jr.*, ed. James Melvin Washington (New York: HarperCollins, 1986), 142.

78. Martin Luther King Jr., "Eulogy for the Martyred Children," in *Testament of Hope*, 221-23.

79. Fannie Lou Hamer, "Sick and Tired of Being Sick and Tired," *Katallagete*, Fall 1968, 26; Fred Hobson, *But Now I See: the White Southern Racial Conversion Narrative* (Baton Rouge: Louisiana State University Press, 1999), 17.

80. Anne Moody, *Coming of Age in Mississippi* (New York: Dial Press, 1968), 60, 255.

81. Ibid., 271, 336.

82. Ibid., 285.

Index

abolitionism, 74, 79, 80, 82–83, 91
abortion issue in the modern South, 10
Abraham, and African Americans, 105
Absalom, Absalom! (Faulkner): backstory of, 38; and the black image in the white mind, 42–43; and evangelicalism, 4, 41–42; incest theme in, 38–39; miscegenation theme in, 39–40; predetermined tragedy of, 36–40; as redemption story, 13, 27; and southern hypocrisy, 40–41
Absalom story (biblical): and evangelicalism, 4; in the slave south, 13–16, 27; and the soul of man, 13; and southern hypocrisy, 5; in southern literature, 36
Adams, John, 6
African Americans: and Abraham, 105; antebellum religious expression of, 16, 17–18, 20–23; the Bible as a "Talking Book" for, 20; and Black Muslims, 145; and Black Panthers, 156; debate over the soul of, 15; devil folklore of, 31–32; encounter with seventeenth- and eighteenth-century Christianity, 57; and the gospel of uplift, 124; and Jesus, 24–26, 68, 99, 100–101, 107; ministries to, 75; Protestant Christianity of, 9, 10, 71–73; providentialism of, 91, 93; religious imagery of, 31. *See also* slavery and slave Christianity
African Methodist Episcopal (AME) Church, 114
Alabama, Protestantism in, 7, 9
Albermarle County, Virginia, 10
"All I Want Is the Pure Religion, Hallelu" (Jefferson), 123
"Amazing Grace" (song), 100
AME (African Methodist Episcopal Church), 114
American Recordings (Cash), 130
American Religious Identification Survey (ARIS), 7, 8f
American Revolution, 101
America's God (Noll), 56
Amite County, Mississippi, 9, 10
Anglican Church, 61, 62, 67, 68
Anglo-American Protestantism: compatibility of slavery and Christianity in, 54–55, 58–59; concentrations in the modern South, 9; dominance in southern religious history, 4; and individual religious liberty, 55–57; and slave conversions, 59–62, 63–66, 68–72, 74–75, 103

173

Apostle, The (film), 96–97
Apostle Paul, 81, 83, 152
Appeal (Walker), 89, 91, 93
ARIS (American Religious Identification Survey), 7, 8f
Asbury, Francis, 74
"Aunt Katy," 21–22
Azusa Street revivals, 118

Baptist Belt, 8f, 9
Baptists: antislavery sentiments of, 74; on miscegenation, 149–50; in the modern South, 7; parallels with native African religion, 69
Barnett, Ross, 149–50
Barton, Bruce, *The Man Nobody Knows*, 113
Battle of Chancellorsville, 20
"Beast in Me" (Cash), 130
Beaufort County, North Carolina, 33
Behold the Man (Johnson), 136, 140, 141
Beloved (Morrison): as Absalom story, 27, 46–48; backstory of, 44; and the black image in the white mind, 48–49; Trickster theme in, 44–47
Berends, Kurt, 19
Berlin, Isaiah, 95
Bible: inspired view of, 10; Moses and Exodus as prototype of the slave experience, 16–19; narratives used as justification for slavery, 16–17, 18–19, 26, 77–82, 83–86; scriptural references, 36, 77; and social conservatism, 83–86; as a "Talking Book" for African Americans, 20
Bible Belt, 6–7, 8f, 9, 10, 99, 100–101
Birmingham, Alabama, 148, 152–53, 156
Birth of a Nation (Griffith), 113, 114
black Americans. *See* African Americans

Black Christ on a Cross (Hunter), 136, *138*
"Black Diamond Express to Hell" (Nix), 133
black evangelical Christianity. *See* African Americans; slavery and slave Christianity
black Jesus: in the arts, 133–34, *135*, 136, *137*–40, 141, *142*–43, 144–45; and black southerners, 125–27, 132–33, 145–49; and the civil rights movement, 100–101, 131–32; and the deracialized Christ, 132–33; in music, 133–34; and the Pentecostal message, 118, 120; as suffering servant, 107; and the white Christ, 114–16; white southerners' reaction to, 144
Black Jesus (Young), 141, *143*
Black Jesus, on a Cross with Figures, White Flowers, and Birds (Hunter), 136
black magic, 27–31
Black Man, the Father of Civilization, The (Webb), 115–16
Black Muslims, 145, 156
Black Panthers, 156
blues music. *See* gospel and blues music
Blum, Edward J., 35–36
Bowers, Sam, 150
"The Boy Who Painted Christ Black" (Clarke), 144
Brown, Henry "Box," *Narrative of Henry Box Brown, Who Escaped from Slavery Enclosed in a Box 3 Feet Long and 2 Wide*, 102
Brown, William Wells, 33–34
Browne, Martha Griffith, 103
Bryan, Hugh, 68

"Caleb Mayer" (Welch), 34–35
Callahan, Allen, 20, 24
Campbell, Lucie, 121
Canty (Morgan), 141

Cash, Johnny, 12, 97, 98, 128–31; *American Recordings*, 130; "Beast in Me," 130; *Johnny Cash at Folsom Prison*, 129; *Johnny Cash at San Quentin Prison*, 129; *Man in Black*, 130; *The Mind of the South*, 97; "Personal Jesus," 131; "Redemption," 130, 131
Cash, June Carter, 129
Cash, Wilbur J., 2, 15, 52, 97, 98
Catholicism, 10, 67, 69, 102
Channing, William Ellery, 82
Charleston, South Carolina, 68
Chase, Lucy, 105
Chicago Defender (newspaper), 115
Christian, William, 118
"Christian Doctrine of Slavery, The " (Thornwell), 81–82
Christian Workers for Fellowship (the Church of the Living God), 118
Christ in the Camp (Jones), 101, 109–10, 112
"Christ Our Starting Point" (King), 148
Church of Christ, Holiness, 117
Church of England. *See* Anglican Church
Church of God, 118
Church of God in Christ, 117
Church of the Living God, the (Christian Workers for Fellowship), 118
civil rights movement: and activist Jesus, 57–58, 154–57; and black Jesus, 100–101, 131–32; and the deracialized Christ, 132–33; and Jesus before the cross, 150–51; and the Jesus of the disinherited, 145–49, 152–54; nonviolence principle of, 147–48; and private segregation, 149–50, 151
Civil War: and conjure men, 29; Jesus as a warrior, 107, 108–9; and the sacralization of the South, 11; and the story of Moses, 18, 19–20
Clansman, The (Dixon), 99–100
Clarke, Erskine, *Dwelling Place*, 54
Clarke, John Henrik, "The Boy Who Painted Christ Black," 144
Clayborn, Edward, "This Time Another Year You May Be Gone," 121
Color Purple, The (Walker), 101, 127
Coming of Age in Mississippi (Moody), 154–56
Cone, James, 145
Confederate camp revivals, 109
Confessions of Nat Turner (Gray), 88
conjure men, 27–31
Constitutional Whig, 88
"Coo Coo Bird" (folk song), 34
Cotton Crucifixion (Hunter), 136, 139
Criswell, W. A., 149
Crucifixion with Red Zinnias (Hunter), 136, 137
Cullen, Countee, 133

Dailey, Jane, 149
Daniel, John W., 111
Davies, Samuel, 68–69
Davis, Gary, 32
Davis, Noah, 103
Davis, Sam, 111
DeBow's Review, 80–81
democratic evangelicalism, 54–58
Democratization of American Christianity, The (Hatch), 56
"Denomination Blues" (Phillips), 122
Derricks, Cleavant, "Just a Little Talk with Jesus," 128
devil, the, as the Trickster, 31–32
Dickinson, Emmett, 123
divorce rates, in the modern South, 12
Dixon, Thomas, 112–13; *The Clansman*, 99–100; "The Larger Church," 113
Dorsey, Thomas A., "How 'bout You?," 121–22; "If You See My Saviour," 122

Douglass, Frederick, 91–93, 100
Du Bois, W. E. B., 100, 133, 141
Duvall, Robert, 96–97
Dwelling Place (Clarke), 54

educational levels, in the modern South, 12
Elfstrom, Robert, 129
Evangelical Belt, 7, 8f, 9, 10
evangelical Christianity, white southern: and antebellum black Christianity, 75–77; antebellum spread of, 41–42; contemporary scholarship on, 4; and democratic evangelicalism, 54–58; dissociation from whiteness, 59; evangelical synthesis of Christianity and slavery, 80–82, 93–95, 97; and the gospel of uplift, 124; as ideology of the master class, 75; and Jesus, 98, 99, 100–101, 107–14; and missions to slaves, 62–65; religious experience of, 13–16; and repression, 57; rise of, 11; and scientific racism, 58–61; and slave converts, 59–62, 65–67, 68–72, 74–75, 103; and social conservatism, 80–86; and the soul of man, 2–3; statistics, 9–11. *See also* slavery and slave Christianity
Exodus, biblical, 17

Faulkner, William, 2, 97–98; *Absalom, Absalom!*, 13, 27, 36–44, 53; *Light in August*, 141; *The Sound and the Fury*, 43–44
Finney, Charles Grandison, 93
First Baptist Church of Dallas, 149
First Baptist Church of Jackson, 149
First Great Awakening, 57, 58, 60, 68–74
First South Carolina Volunteers, 105
Fletcher, John, 78
Floyd, John, 89–90

Forten, Charles, 105
Fort Mose, Florida, 66
Frazier, E. Franklin, 141; *Negro Youth at the Crossways*, 131
Freedom's Coming (Harvey), 4
freedom songs, 120
French and Indian War, 69

Gabriel's Rebellion, 64
Gallup Poll, 10–11
Garner, Margaret, 44
Garnet, Henry Highland, 93
Garrison, William Lloyd, 80, 89
Garvey, Marcus, 114
Gates, William, *Little Black Train Is Coming*, 133
Genesis 9:18–27, used as justification for slavery, 77
Genovese, Elizabeth Fox, *Mind of the Master Class*, 79
Genovese, Eugene, *Mind of the Master Class*, 79
Glorious Revolution of 1688, 60
"Go Down Moses" (black spiritual), 90
God Struck Me Dead (Pilgrim Press), 125
Goldwyn, Morgan, 59
Gone with the Wind (film), 97
gospel and blues music, 31–33, 116–17, 120–23, 127–29, 133. *See also* hymns and spirituals
Gospel Road, The (film), 129
Gospel Train, The (Graham), 133
Grace, C. M. "Daddy," 136
Graham, Lemuel, *The Gospel Train*, 133
Grant, Madison, *The Passing of the Great Race*, 113
Gray, Thomas R., 90; *Confessions of Nat Turner*, 88
Great Awakening. *See* First Great Awakening; Second Great Awakening
Green, John, 10

176 Index

Griffith, D. W., *Birth of a Nation*, 113, 114
Ground of Truth church, 118
gun violence rates, in the modern South, 12

Hadley, Elder J. J. *See* Patton, Charley
Hamer, Fannie Lou, 153–54, 156
Hampton, Wade, 112
Harvey, Paul, *Freedom's Coming*, 4
Hatch, Nathan, *The Democratization of American Christianity*, 56
Head of Christ (Sallman), 133, 144, 145
Heyrman, Christine, *Southern Cross*, 11
Higginson, Thomas Wentworth, 105–6
Highlander Folk School, 99
"High Water Rising" (Patton), 33
Holiness/Pentecostalism, black southern, 116–18
hoodoo, 27–31
Hopkins, Dwight, 26
Horton, Miles, 99
House, Eddie James "Son," Jr., 12
"How 'bout You?" (Dorsey), 121–22
Hudgins, Douglas, 149–50
Hunter, Clementine, *Black Christ on a Cross*, 136, *138*; *Black Jesus, on a Cross with Figures, White Flowers, and Birds*, 136; *Cotton Crucifixion*, 136, *139*; *Crucifixion with Red Zinnias*, 136, *137*
Hunter, W. L., *Jesus Christ Had Negro Blood in His Veins*, 116
Hurston, Zora Neale, 125–26
hymns and spirituals, 17, 20–21, 90–91, 116–18, 120, 121. *See also* gospel and blues music

"If You See My Saviour" (Dorsey), 122
"I Have a Dream" (King), 152

"I'm Goin to Bury Myself in Jesus's Arms" (gospel), 121
Indian conversion to Christianity, 63
infant mortality rates, in the modern South, 12
Invisible Empire of the Second Klu Klux Klan, 113–14, 150, 152–53
Irony of Southern History, The (Woodward), 13
"I Saw the Light" (Williams), 128
Islam, 58

"Jack of Diamonds" (folk song), 34
Jackson, Cordelia, 102–3
Jackson, Stonewall, 20
James, Nehemiah "Skip," 32; "Jesus Is a Mighty Leader," 120–21
Jefferson, Blind Lemon, 32, 121; "All I Want Is the Pure Religion, Hallelu," 123; "Low Down Mojo Blues," 32; "Please See My Grave Is Kept Clean," 123
Jefferson, Thomas, 6, 55–56, 93
"Jemmy" (leader of slave rebellion), 67
Jesus: as activist, 57–58, 154–57; and African Americans, 24–26, 68, 99, 100–101, 107; before the cross, 150–51; in black southern theology, 125–27, 132–33, 145–49; of the civil rights movement, 100–101, 131–32; as Civil War warrior, 107–9; Confederate stand-ins for, 111; deracialized, 131–32; of the disinherited, 145–49, 152–54; emergence in American history of, 101; imagery of, 3, 22–24, 99–100, 103–4, 113, 125–26, 127, 129, 131; in the interwar years, 133; as king, 24–26, 68, 105, 121; and the Klu Klux Klan, 113–14; patron saint of the Lost and Redemptionist Causes, 98, 99, 100–101, 107–14; as a radical figure, 98–101; as a second Moses, 3, 17, 121–24;

Jesus (continued)
  slave encounters with, 21–23; in the slave south, 13–16, 20–23, 26–27, 68–69, 98, 101–6; and the soul of man, 1, 13; and train symbolism, 122–23, 133–34; as a trickster of the trinity, 5, 35–36, 124, 130; in white southern working-class theology, 124–25. See also black Jesus
Jesus and the Disinherited (Thurman), 132
Jesus and the Three Marys (Johnson), 134, 135
Jesus Christ Had Negro Blood in His Veins (Hunter), 116
"Jesus Is All" (gospel), 121
"Jesus Is a Mighty Leader" (James), 120–21
"Jesus Is Getting Us Ready for That Great Day" (Magby), 121
Jesus Only (Jones), 117–18
"Jesus Was Our Savior—Cotton Was Our King" (Shaver), 130
"Jesus Will Make It Alright" (gospel), 121
Job (book of the Bible), 18
Joe Turner Come and Gone (Wilson), 127
Johnny Cash at Folsom Prison (album), 129
Johnny Cash at San Quentin Prison (album), 129
Johns, Vernon, 150–51
Johnson, Anderson, *Behold the Man*, 136, 140, 141
Johnson, Blind Willie, 1, 122; "John the Revelator," 1; "What Is the Soul of Man?," 1, 2, 12–13
Johnson, Robert, 32
Johnson, William H., *Jesus and the Three Marys*, 134, 135
"John the Revelator" (Johnson), 1
Jones, Charles Colcock, 28–29, 54–55, 76–77, 87; *The Religious Instruction of Negroes in the United States*, 54
Jones, Charles Price, *Jesus Only*, 117–18
Jones, Edward P., 2; *The Known World*, 27, 49–52
Jones, George, 128
Jones, John William, *Christ in the Camp*, 101, 109–110, 112
Jones, Thomas, 71
Jordan, Winthrop, 77–78
Judaism, 9
"Just a Little Talk with Jesus" (Derricks), 128

Kelsey, George D., 146
Kentucky, 7, 12
Kester, Howard, 99
King, Martin Luther, Jr., 145–48, 150, 151–54; "Christ Our Starting Point," 148; "I Have a Dream," 152; "Letter from a Birmingham Jail," 152
Kingdom of Kongo, 67
King Jesus, 24–26, 68, 105, 121
Known World, The (Jones), 27, 49–52
Ku Klux Klan, and the Invisible Empire, 113–14, 150, 152–53

Lacy, Rubin, 32
"Larger Church, The" (Dixon), 113
Las Vegas, Nevada, 12
Law of Servants and Slaves (Virginia, 1705), 60
Lee, Jerena, 45
Lee, Robert E., 108, 111–12
Le Jau, Francis, 62–64, 64–65
Lenoir, J. B., 32
"Letter from a Birmingham Jail" (King), 152
Levine, Lawrence, 28
Lewis, Jerry Lee, 127–28
Lewis, John, 98, 148–49
Light in August (Faulkner), 141

Lincoln, Abraham, 18
literacy skills survey, 12
Little Black Train Is Coming (Gates), 133
"Long Black Veil" (ballad), 35
Longstreet, James, 111
Lost Cause, the, 11, 99–100, 107
Louisiana, 12
"Love That Forgives, The" (sermon), 152
"Low Down Mojo Blues" (Jefferson), 32
Lowery, Joseph, 145–46
Ludlam, Richard, 65
"Luke the Drifter" (Williams), 35, 128
Lynch, Mildred, 108

Madison, James, 55
Magby, Luther, "Jesus Is Getting Us Ready for That Great Day," 121
mainline Protestantism, in the modern South, 7, 9
Man in Black (Cash), 130
Manley, Sarah, 108
Man Nobody Knows, The (Barton), 113
March on Washington (1963), 151
Marrant, John, 71–72
Maryland, 59
Mason, Charles Harrison, 117, 118, 119, 120
Mays, Benjamin, 147; *The Negro's God, as Reflected in His Literature*, 131
McTell, Blind Willie, 32
Meade, William, 101
MEC (Methodist Episcopal Church), 74
Mencken, H. L., 52
Menendez, Francisco, 66
Methodist Episcopal Church (MEC), 74
Methodists, 9, 70, 73, 74–75
Mind of the Master Class (Genovese and Genovese), 79
Mind of the South, The (Cash), 97

Mississippi, 7, 9, 12, 153
Mississippi River, flood of 1927, 33
modern South: abortion issue in, 10; Baptists in, 7; bifurcated soul of, 12–13; contradictions of, 14–16; divorce rates in, 12; educational levels in, 12; gun violence rates in, 12; infant mortality rates in, 12; mainline Protestantism in, 7, 9; murder rates in, 12; negative social indices of, 11–12; non-Christian percentage in, 10; obesity rates in, 12
Monroe, Bill, 128
Montgomery Bus Boycott, 146, 148
Moody, Anne, *Coming of Age in Mississippi*, 154–56
Moore, Gatemouth, 32
moral establishment, the, 3
Morgan, Gertrude: *Canty*, 141; *Self-Portrait in White with Jesus*, 141, 142
Mormons, 9
Morrison, Toni, 2; *Beloved*, 27, 44, 46–49
Moses: and the Civil War, 18, 19–20; and Exodus as prototype of the slave experience, 16–19; and Jesus, 3, 17, 121–24; political rhetoric and the story of, 16; in the slave south, 3, 5, 13–16, 18–21, 26–27; and the soul of man, 13; in the white southern mythos, 18–21, 26–27
Moses, Bob, 155
Moses, Patsy, 29
murder rates, in the modern South, 12
Myth of American Religious Freedom, The (Sehat), 2

Narrative of Henry Box Brown, Who Escaped from Slavery Enclosed in a Box 3 Feet Long and 2 Wide (Brown), 102

Negro's God, as Reflected in His Literature, The (Mays), 131
Negro Youth at the Crossways (Frazier), 131
Nevada, 12
New Deal era, 99
New England, as the Bible Belt, 6–7
New Light Christianity, 68
New Testament, and slavery, 19
New York, 66
New York Tract Society, 89
Niebuhr, Reinhold, 99
Nix, A. W., "Black Diamond Express to Hell," 133
Noll, Mark, 79–80; *America's God*, 56
North American Religious Atlas, 7, 9
North Star (periodical), 91

obesity rates, in the modern South, 12
"O Death" (folk song), 34
Oklahoma, 12
Old Testament and slavery, 16–17, 18–19, 26, 77–82, 83–86
Orange County, Virginia, 110

Palmer, Benjamin Morgan, 85
Passing of the Great Race, The (Grant), 113
Patton, Charley (pseud. Elder J. J. Hadley), 122; "High Water Rising," 33; "Prayer of Death," 131
Paul (apostle), 81, 83, 152
Pentecostalism, 27, 118, 120
Perkins, Carl, 128
"Personal Jesus" (Cash), 131
Philips, Ulrich B., 15
Phillips, Washington, "Denomination Blues," 122
Pierce, Elijah, 136
Pillar church, the, 118
Pine Ridge Indian Reservation, 12
"Please See My Grave Is Kept Clean" (Jefferson), 123

"Poor Wayfaring Stranger" (folk song), 34
Powdermaker, Hortense, 30
"Prayer of Death," (Patton), 131
"Precious Lord Take My Hand" (gospel), 121
premillenialism, 93
Presley, Elvis, 128
"Pretty Polly" (ballad), 35
prose literacy skills survey, 12
Protestant African American Christianity, 9, 10, 71–73
Protestant evangelical Christianity, 2–3, 4, 55–57
providentialism, African American, 91, 93
Puritans, 101

Quakers, 60, 105

racial segregation, 99, 113, 149–50, 151
Randolph, Peter, 104
Rankin, Thomas, 70
"Rank Strangers" (folk song), 34
"Redemption" (Cash), 130, 131
Religion and Public Life in the South (Religion by Religion series), 7
Religious Herald, 110
religious importance survey, 10–11
Religious Instruction of Negroes in the United States, The (Jones), 54
republican providentialism, 80–82, 93–95
revivalism, 93, 109–10
Revivalists, 70
Richmond, Virginia, 71
Rockingham County, Virginia, 34
Rural Negro, The (Woodson), 126

Sallman, Walter, *Head of Christ*, 133, 144, 145
Saving Grace (television), 100–101
scientific racism, 58–61

Second Great Awakening, 55, 57, 93, 101
secularists, 10
segregation, racial, 99, 113, 149–50, 151
Sehat, David, *The Myth of American Religious Freedom*, 2
Self-Portrait in White with Jesus (Morgan), 141, *142*
Separate Baptists, 70
"Seven Sister Blues" (Smith), 29
Seven Sisters, 29
Shaver, Billy Joe, "Jesus Was Our Savior—Cotton Was Our King," 130
Sherman, William T., 17
Shuttlesworth, Fred, 152
Simmons, William J., 113
"Sinner You'll Need King Jesus" (Smith and Smith), 121
Sixteenth Street Baptist Church, 148, 152–53, 156
slavery and slave Christianity: and abolitionism, 74, 79, 80, 82–83, 91; biblical defense of, 16–17, 18–19, 26, 77–82, 83–86; conversion of slaves, 59–63, 64–66, 68–72, 74–75, 103; Genesis 9:18–27 used as justification for slavery, 77; identification with the children of Israel, 17–18; and Jesus, 13–16, 20–23, 26–27, 68–69, 98, 101–6; and native African religions, 58; rebellions and uprisings, 64–65, 65–67, 71, 82, 86, 87–90; runaway slaves, 70–71; slave preachers, 86–90; and social conservatism, 80–86; and the soul of man debate, 1–5, 12–13, 15–16, 58–59; spirituals of, 17, 20–21, 90–91. *See also* evangelical Christianity, white southern
Smith, J. T. "Funny Papa," "Seven Sister Blues," 29

Smith, Lillian, 98
Smith, Versey, "Sinner You'll Need King Jesus," 121
Smith, William, "Sinner You'll Need King Jesus," 121
SNCC (Student Nonviolent Coordinating Committee), 156
social conservatism, 80–86
Society for the Propagation of the Gospel in Foreign Parts (SPG), 58, 62–63
son-of-Ham racial theology, 77–78
Sons of Confederate Veterans, 109
soul music, 120
soul of man debate, 1–5, 12–13, 15–16, 58–59
Sound and the Fury, The (Faulkner), 43–44
South Carolina, 62, 66, 68, 74
South Dakota, 12
Southern Baptist Convention, 108
Southern Christian Leadership Conference, 152
Southern Cross (Heyrman), 11
Southern Harmony (hymnal), 34
southern religious history, contemporary scholarship in, 4
Spencer, Jon, 32, 33
SPG (Society for the Propagation of the Gospel in Foreign Parts), 58, 62–63
spirituals. *See* hymns and spirituals
Stamps-Baxter Company, 128
St. Augustine, Florida, 66
"Steal Away to Jesus" (slave spiritual), 21
Stone Mountain, Georgia, 113
Stono River Rebellion, 64, 67
Stowe, Harriet Beecher, *Uncle Tom's Cabin*, 45, 79
Stringfellow, Lawrence, 81
Strychasz, Jennifer, 133
Student Nonviolent Coordinating Committee (SNCC), 156
Sundquist, Eric, 42

Tennessee, 7, 12
Tharpe, Sister Rosetta, 121
"This Time Another Year You May Be Gone" (Clayborn), 121
Thomas, Ella Gertrude Clanton, 107
Thomas, Henry, 123
Thornwell, James Henley, 81–82, 83, 85, 149; "The Christian Doctrine of Slavery," 81–82
Thurman, Howard, *Jesus and the Disinherited*, 132
Tindley, Charles Albert, 121
train symbolism, and Jesus, 122–23, 133–34
Travis, Joseph, 21
Traylor, Bill, 136
Trickster: in blues lyrics, 31–33; conjure men as, 27–31; as a defining theme of southern religion, 4, 13–16, 27–28; the Devil as, 31–32; Jesus as, 5, 35–36, 124, 130; and the soul of man, 13; in white folklore and music, 33–35
Tucker, John Randolph, 20
Tunstal, Harris, 112
Turner, Henry McNeal, 114–15, 116, 144, 145; *Voice of Missions*, 114–15
Turner, Nat, 66, 72, 80, 86–88, 89–90, 93
"Two Railroads to Eternity" (sermon visual aid), 133

Uncle Tom's Cabin (Stowe), 45, 79
United Church of Prayer for all People, 136
United Confederate Veterans, 112
United Daughters of the Confederacy, 109

United Klans of America, 152–53

Vance, James I., 108
Varnod, Francis, 66
Vesey, Denmark, 64, 82
Virginia, 9–10, 58, 59–60, 110
Voice of Missions (Turner), 114–15
voodoo, 27–31

Walker, Alice, *The Color Purple*, 101, 127
Walker, David, 116; *Appeal*, 89, 91, 93
Watkins, James, 103
Webb, James Morrison, *The Black Man, the Father of Civilization*, 115–16
Welch, Gillian, "Caleb Mayer," 34–35
Wesley, John, 73
West Virginia, 12
"What Is the Soul of Man?" (Johnson), 1, 2, 12–13
Wheetstraw, Peetie, 32
White Citizens' Council, 148
Whitefield, George, 68, 71
white folklore and music, and the Trickster, 33–35
Whitfield, Owen, 98, 99
Williams, Carlos, 125
Williams, Hank, "I Saw the Light," 128; "Luke the Drifter," 35, 128
Wilson, August, *Joe Turner Come and Gone*, 127
Woodson, Carter, *The Rural Negro*, 126
Woodward, C. Vann, *The Irony of Southern History*, 13

Young, Purvis, *Black Jesus*, 141

Selected Books from the Mercer University Lamar Memorial Lectures

※

The Brown *Decision, Jim Crow, and Southern Identity*
James C. Cobb

Teaching Equality: Black Schools in the Age of Jim Crow
Adam Fairclough

Becoming Confederates: Paths to a New National Loyalty
Gary W. Gallagher

A Consuming Fire: The Fall of the Confederacy in the Mind of the White Christian South
Eugene D. Genovese

Moses, Jesus, and the Trickster in the Evangelical South
Paul Harvey

George Washington and the American Military Tradition
Don Higginbotham

South to the Future: An American Region in the Twenty-First Century
Edited by Fred Hobson

The Countercultural South
Jack Temple Kirby

Singing Cowboys and Musical Mountaineers: Southern Culture and the Roots of Country Music
Bill C. Malone

"Mixed Blood" Indians: Racial Construction in the Early South
Theda Perdue

Camille, 1969: Histories of a Hurricane
Mark M. Smith

Weathering the Storm: Inside Winslow Homer's Gulf Stream
Peter H. Wood

www.ingramcontent.com/pod-product-compliance
Lightning Source LLC
Chambersburg PA
CBHW010927180426
43192CB00043B/2786